THE STABLE OF EDDIE THOMAS

Class of the 60s

First published in Great Britain in 2005 by

Wynford Jones
3, Sycamore Close,
Aberdare

© Wynford Jones, who has asserted his right to be identified as the author of this work.

Printed and bound by
Colourplan Design and Print
St Helens
Merseyside.

A catalogue record for this book
is available from the British Library.

ISBN 0-9551082-0-9

Gloucestershire County Library	
9925O9813 O	
Askews	16-Mar-2006
796.83	£12.95

CONTENTS

Acknowledgements vii

Introduction viii

A Tribute to Eddie Thomas by John Lloyd x

Chapter 1 Eddie Thomas 1

Chapter 2 Howard Winstone 17

Chapter 3 Eddie Avoth 29

Chapter 4 Ken Buchanan 37

Chapter 5 Gerald Jones 49

Chapter 6 Carl Gizzi 53

Chapter 7 Glyn Davies 61

Chapter 8 Roger Tighe 67

Chapter 9 Gordon Davies 71

Chapter 10 Malcolm Price 75

Chapter 11 Dai Gardiner 79

Chapter 12 Dai Harris 85

Chapter 13 John Gamble 91

Chapter 14 Don James 99

Chapter 15 Stuart Price 105

Chapter 16 Gerry Banwell 109

Chapter 17 Roy John 113

Chapter 18 Allan Ball 119

Chapter 19 Dennis Avoth 123

Chapter 20 Recollections of the stable 129

ACKNOWLEDGEMENTS

I am extremely grateful to John Lloyd for agreeing to write a tribute to Eddie Thomas for this book. As a Merthyr man who went on to become Welsh Sports Editor for the Daily Express for thirty years, John wrote at length on the achievements of Eddie Thomas and his stable of boxers, and for me, was the ideal person for the task.

Many of the photographs used in this book were taken by Tommy Rees of Seer Sports in Cardiff. He was a regular visitor to the gym taking promotional pictures of the boxers and was an ever-present figure at ringside.

I am grateful to the Western Mail and Echo for the use of photographs and special thanks go to Tony Woolway, Grant Bicknell and Saffron Herbert for their help. I would also like to thank the Daily Express for the use of their photographs. Every effort has been made to acknowledge copyright and I can only apologise in cases where it was impossible to establish the copyright holder.

I am also grateful to Gareth and his staff at Victoria Studios, Aberdare, for their help with photographic material.

Thanks go to Claude Abrams, the Editor of Boxing News, whose record books and annuals proved invaluable in compiling the career records of all the boxers featured in the book.

Special mention goes to Don James, Secretary of the Welsh Ex-Boxers' Association who has always been happy to talk about the great days at the gym and has been a constant support.

Finally, I would like to thank Brian and Doreen Meadows for their help. Some time ago I commissioned a painting of Eddie Thomas from them and they have kindly allowed me to use this in the cover design. Brian's assistance has also been invaluable in helping me see this book through to publication.

Wynford Jones

INTRODUCTION

On February 28th, 2003, members of the Eddie Thomas stable of the 60's gathered at the Bessemer Hotel, Dowlais, for what was an eagerly awaited re-union.

The evening was organised by Don James, secretary of the Welsh Ex-Boxers' Association and himself a distinguished member of the stable. People travelled from all over Britain to be present and as President of the Welsh Ex-Boxers' Association, I had the honour of introducing all the stable members. There was a great sense of drama as the sound of a fanfare greeted the appearance of the boxers and there was a special moment when they were all finally on stage, as they stood shoulder to shoulder for some photographs together.

Stable members present were introduced as follows:
Chris Collins: Sparring partner to Don James and Gerald Jones. One of the first boxers to appear on TV.
Ken Jones: British Boys' Clubs Champion.
Billy Gardner: Welsh International and Railways Champion.
Billy O'Donovan: One of the first members of the stable.
Colin Davies: Welsh International.
Gordon Davies: Welsh ABA Featherweight Champion, 1961. Drew with Teddy Best for Welsh Lightweight Title in 1963.
Dai Gardiner: Welsh ABA Lightweight Champion, 1962. Manager of Johnny Owen, Robbie Regan and Steve Robinson emulating the achievements of his former manager, Eddie Thomas.
Johnny Gamble: Welsh and ABA Lightmiddleweight Champion, 1961 and British NCB champion.
Dave "Pen" Jones: Boxed in the Welsh Championships.
Malcolm Price: One of the founder members of the stable and a Welsh International.
Johnny Harris: A founder member of the stable and long-standing amateur trainer.
Don James: Welsh ABA Flyweight Champion in 1960. British NCB Champ. Beat future world champion Walter McGowan. Don is the driving force behind the Welsh Ex-Boxers' Association and worked hard on the Howard Winstone statue appeal fund.
Gerald Jones: Welsh ABA Flyweight Champion, 1961. As a pro in 1966 he became Welsh Bantamweight Champion beating Terry Gale in eight rounds at Aberavon. Now a successful and respected trainer at Dowlais ABC.

Roy John: Welsh ABA Lightheavyweight Champion, 1965. Challenged Chris Finnegan in 1973 for the British Lightheavyweight Title.

Colin Lake: Sparring partner to Howard Winstone and highly respected trainer of former WBU Lightweight Champion, Colin "Dynamo" Dunne.

Eddie Avoth: Welsh ABA Lightmiddleweight Champion, 1963. In 1969, he became British Lightheavyweight Champion and beat Trevor Thornbury in Brisbane to become Empire Champion.

Ken Buchanan: MBE. Came to train in Merthyr and went on to become British, World and European Lightweight Champion. In 2000, he was inducted into the International Boxing Hall of Fame, the "Tartan Legend".

Later in the evening, Don James, Ken Buchanan, Eddie Avoth and Dai Gardiner told interesting stories about their time together in the gym and each paid tribute to the contribution of Eddie Thomas. There was a fascinating question and answer session predictably laced with humour and everyone present responded to this while all the guests willingly signed autographs and posed for photographs.

Everyone had come together like one large family and it was a joy to see young Eddie and Geraint Thomas with Wayne and young Howard Winstone present to cement the connection with the past.

It was well after midnight when people began to disperse, reluctantly, for it had been one of those rare occasions which will live on in the memory, made all the more memorable by some very special people, the "Class of the 60s."

As time passed, I began to think about what the evening meant to me and how the friendships made during that time have lasted to the present day. I began to realise that I had witnessed something unique and how the experience of watching these men punish their bodies in preparation for action in the ring had influenced my own involvement in boxing, which has brought me immense pleasure.

What follows is a personal look back at those days and the boxers who turned professional during the course of the decade under the tutelage of the maestro himself, Eddie Thomas. I have taken Eddie's own career as my starting point, leading on to the boxers who not only made a great impression on me, but who also made such an impact in the toughest of sports.

A TRIBUTE TO EDDIE THOMAS
by **John Lloyd**
Former Merthyr Express and Daily Express Welsh Sports Editor

"The simplest way to know Merthyr Tydfil is to know Eddie Thomas"

Those immortal words were written by Sunday newspaper ace sports columnist Hugh McIlvanney in his best selling book "McIlvanney on Boxing" (1996). "Mac the Words" took you every inch of the colourful highways and byways as the modest, home-loving Colliers Row boy masterminded fellow townsman Howard Winstone and Scot Ken Buchanan to world crowns and went agonisingly close to a dazzling hat-trick with Colin Jones.

On the home front, it was King Edward first on the tragic scene of the Aberfan Disaster and one of the last to be dragged away. McIlvanney saluted him like this: "There is so much that is exceptional about Eddie, coal miner son of a coal miner, outstanding welterweight champion of his time. He is a giant in the working class mythology of Merthyr."

"It was natural that he should have been found using the skills learned underground to extricate with tender patience, many of the small bodies buried by the avalanche of slurry."

Merthyr's hard fight for a place in the worldwide economic sun after the Industrial Revolution inspired Our Ed. At after-fight inquests at London's Regent Palace Hotel, he would wax lyrical about the first-class iron made in the Dowlais and Cyfarthfa Ironworks clinching Britain's defeat of the Spanish Armada. He was also eloquent about Nye Bevan basing his blueprint for the National Health Service on life in the Rhymney and Merthyr Valleys.

Maybe our lives hinge on being at the right place at the right time. Punctuality was not one of Eddie's attributes! Ken Buchanan brought his parents to Merthyr to meet Eddie before the bright, much-sought-after

Scot turned professional in the highly competitive Big Boxing world. They arrived for a 6pm rendezvous at the New Inn. I was among the small welcoming committee running out of excuses for what had delayed Eddie. Finally, breathless, ever-busy Ed arrived, more than an hour late. The philanthropic promoter had been delivering free coal and boxing tickets in between hospital visits and council work! The kitchen had closed but Eddie charmed the hotel staff into re-opening and entertained the Buchanan clan with "I Have Heard The Mavis Singing, Its Love Song To The Morn" as their well-done steaks were cooked.

Mrs Buchanan admitted: "We've been shown around London, and royally looked after by promoter-matchmaker Mickey Duff, but its homely Merthyr we want for our son! Merthyr definitely!"

Ken and manager, trainer - cutsman Eddie were also in the right place, namely Madison Square Garden, New York at the right time. Ken's world title looked like ebbing away with a badly swollen eye against Ismael Laguna in 1971. Ice-cool Ed called for a razor blade and "nicked" the injury to release the blood and Ken stayed undisputed Lightweight Champion of the World!

Muhammad Ali`s trainer Angelo Dundee led the chorus of praise for world-class performances by Buchanan and his manager. Even legendary Harold Conrad summed up: "Buchanan's a terrific fighter but I wouldn`t bet he would have won without Thomas!"

The gym at Penydarren to the left with gallery windows.

1

Eddie Thomas

During the 1960s Eddie Thomas nurtured what was at the time, the most successful stable in British boxing, and it was he, more than anyone else, who secured for the town of Merthyr Tydfil its place in the history of boxing.

The town itself was at the centre of the Industrial Revolution and in many ways still bears the scars. There is no doubt that life was hard and people fought to survive, and this constant struggle against the odds provided the ideal breeding ground for what traditionally became known as the "Hungry fighter".

Wales has its tradition of mountain fighters and in the early years of the twentieth century Jimmy Wilde and Tommy Farr were among those who thrived on the apprenticeship which the boxing booths provided. The booths of Jack Scarrott and Joe Guess toured valley communities and developed the talents of countless fighters while in Merthyr itself boxing was synonymous with Snow's Pavilion, and at various times both Wilde and Farr displayed their skills in the town.

During the first half of the twentieth century Merthyr produced many boxers of quality. Because of the intense level of competition some did not progress beyond a Welsh title while Cuthbert Taylor was surely prevented from reaching his full potential because of the colour bar which remained in force until the British Boxing Board of Control changed its policy in 1948, two years after his retirement from boxing.

Merthyr was able to boast a clutch of remarkable fighting men. Cuthbert Taylor had won the Welsh Bantamweight title but was prevented from progressing further when Wales joined the British Boxing Board of Control after its formation in 1929, but there were other Welsh Champions such as flyweight Jerry O'Neil and bantamweight Dan Dando, while Billy Eynon is said to have taken part in a contest which saw a record attendance approaching 200,000 people while serving in the armed forces in Salonika. It was the achievements of these men which fired the imagination of the young Eddie Thomas as he grew up in this historic town.

Eddie was born at Colliers' Row in Merthyr Tydfil on July 27th, 1926 and was one of six brothers. As a young boy he sang in the choir at Cyfarthfa Church and when he left school he worked for a short time at a gents outfitters. His father and older brothers were inevitably employed in the mining industry and within a short time Eddie decided to join them.

As a young boy, he found the lure of the ring irresistible. He enjoyed a glittering amateur career, frequently boxing several times a week. He won a Welsh ABA junior title in Penarth in 1943 and went on to win the British Bantamweight title. In his first season as a senior he represented Wales and in 1946 he won the Welsh and ABA Lightweight titles. He also represented Great Britain against France in Paris and against the American Golden Gloves team, winning his own contest and contributing to a 5-3 victory. One of his team-mates was Randolph Turpin and they would appear many times together in future years under the promotional banner of Jack Solomons.

Later that year he turned professional with London manager Sam Burns and made his debut on the undercard of the first encounter between Freddie Mills and Bruce Woodcock. He outpointed Ivor Simpson over four rounds and the venue was Harringay Arena, where he would appear many times during his career.

Eddie then went on to register wins over Reg Quinlan in Aberdare and Don Chiswell in Merthyr before appearing at Ninian Park, Cardiff on September 4th on the undercard of the contest between the American Ike Williams and Ronnie James of Swansea for the Lightweight Championship of the World. Eddie beat Bob Ramsey on points over six rounds, but sadly, James was knocked out in the ninth round and had no answer to the devastating body punches of the American.

Eddie tasted defeat for the first time as a professional in his eleventh contest when he was stopped in three rounds by Yrjoe Pitulainen at Harringay but he recovered quickly from this setback with wins over Kid Marcel and Willy Wimms. The name of Kid Marcel would later appear on the record of Sugar Ray Robinson. He was one of Robinson's opponents on his European tour in 1951 and was knocked out in five rounds in Paris on May 21st. Robinson engaged in seven contests between May and July, the final contest of his tour coming against Randolph Turpin at Earls Court on July 10th when he lost his world title to Turpin on points over fifteen rounds. Victory for Turpin secured his place in boxing history, even though his reign as champion was to last a mere sixtyfour days. In the manner of a true champion, Sugar Ray tore back the title when staring defeat in the face. Robinson was badly cut and was within a whisker of defeat, but remarkably, he was able to turn things round with a desperate effort which forced the stoppage.

His first contest in 1948 saw Eddie matched with Sheffield's Henry Hall at the Royal Albert Hall and Thomas emerged with a points decision following a gruelling battle over eight rounds, though the painful effects of Hall's attacks to the body stayed with Eddie for a couple of months.

In March he lost to Gwyn Williams in a British Welterweight title eliminator, but avenged this defeat later in the year and won the Welsh Welterweight title in the process when he outpointed Williams over twelve rounds.

On July 26th, 1948 Eddie was matched with Ernie Roderick, the dominant figure in the Welterweight division almost throughout the 1940's. Roderick was an outright winner of the Lonsdale Belt and in May, 1939, challenged the legendary Henry Armstrong for the world title only to lose on points over fifteen rounds. In only his eighteenth contest, Eddie beat Roderick on points over eight rounds, but the significance of this result was probably overshadowed by the fact that topping the bill was Freddie Mills, who made it one of British boxing's great nights by defeating Gus Lesnevich on points over fifteen rounds to win the Lightheavyweight Championship of the World, the venue being London's White City.

Eddie rounded off the year with wins over Willie Whyte and Giel de Roode while in 1949 he asserted his true calibre. On February 7th he was matched with the American Billy Graham at Harringay and emerged with an impressive win on points over ten rounds. Graham was already a veteran of seventyseven contests while this was only Eddie's twentythird fight. Graham later went on to beat the Cuban Hawk, Kid Gavilan on points over ten rounds and when he challenged Gavilan for the second time for the world title in Havana, it seems that Billy was the victim of a home-town decision.

In his encounter with Billy Graham, Eddie must have won eight of the ten rounds, dictating the contest with his left hand. By the halfway point Graham's left eye was almost closed and at the final bell the American was quick to acknowledge Eddie's superiority while his delighted supporters sang the Welsh National Anthem and "Sosban Fach".

Another of Billy Graham's former opponents was Carmen Basilio, the former World Welterweight and Middleweight Champion. Basilio, who will be remembered for his epic battles with Tony DeMarco for the welterweight championship and his two fights with Sugar Ray Robinson for the middleweight championship, visited Merthyr recently and I had the honour of introducing him both at the Bessemer Hotel in Dowlais, where he was the guest of honour, and the following night at the Civic Centre in Merthyr when Ken Buchanan was made an Honorary Citizen of the County Borough of Merthyr Tydfil. I was able to talk to Carmen at length and sought his views on Billy Graham. He engaged in a three fight series with Graham resulting in a win, a loss, and a draw. He maintained that Graham was the finest boxer of the time not to have won a world title, and that he had learned so much from their three contests. He praised Graham's chin claiming to have hit him with big punches and Carmen was full of praise for Billy Graham's fighting spirit and competitive nature. In Carmen's words, "he was one tough sonofabitch!".

Eddie then went on to beat Stan Hawthorne in a British title eliminator, a contest which earned him a coveted "Boxing News" Certificate of Merit and in September he faced Ernie Roderick again, but this time over twelve rounds with the contest recognised as another title eliminator. Eddie repeated his earlier victory and the path to the British title was now clear. Henry Hall was by now the British Champion and so they clashed for the second time but with the championship at stake. On November 15th, they met at Harringay over fifteen rounds and Eddie won on points. At the end of the contest Eddie took the microphone and sang "Bless This House" to the fans and this became something of a tradition.

Eddie kept busy through 1950 with contests against continental opposition and defended his title for the first time against Cliff Curvis at St Helen's rugby and cricket ground in Swansea. This turned out to be a disappointing contest with referee Jack Hart frequently having to call for more action. There was much at stake with two Welshmen contesting the title on home soil but at the final bell the referee raised Eddie's arm as the winner on points.

It is interesting to note that many fight reports reflect the frustration of the boxing writers with regard to Eddie's tactics in the ring. He was generally regarded as a slow starter and would only do as much as was required to bring about the victory. They were sometimes dismayed at what they perceived to be his lack of the "killer instinct".

In January, 1951 Eddie travelled to Johannesburg to challenge Pat Patrick for the Empire title. The title had been vacant for twentyfive years after Tommy Milligan relinquished. Previous holders had included Johnny Summers, Matt Wells, Johnny Basham and Ted "Kid" Lewis, one of boxing's true greats. Beforehand, Eddie was acknowledged as the better boxer but there were fears that he might be affected by the altitude if it developed into a long contest. Before a crowd of 13,000 people and in torrential rain, Eddie knocked out Pat Patrick in thirteen rounds to take the title. The South African press was generous in its praise. Vivian Grainger wrote in the Johannesburg "Sunday Express": "He dictated the fight almost throughout with one of the finest left hands ever seen in this country", while Paul Irwin, writing in the Johannesburg "Sunday Times" described the ending thus: (Patrick) was suddenly straightened with a right and then smashed down with a perfect left hook to the jaw. "Patrick went down as though pole-axed and stayed down long beyond the ten second count".

There was no time to savour the fact that he was now British and Empire Champion because just over two weeks later he was back in the ring at the Market Hall in Carmarthen to challenge Michele Palermo for the European title. The Italian was thirtynine years old and had held his national title no less than five times over an eighteen year period but he was vastly experienced and his record showed that he had been stopped only once in 117 contests. Victory in style was essential in view of the speculation regarding a world title fight after Sugar Ray Robinson had recently defeated Jake LaMotta for the World Middleweight title at Chicago Stadium.

Eddie, with his superior boxing skills beat Michele Palermo on points over fifteen rounds and by becoming a triple champion staked his claim as a contender for the World title. Palermo was a rugged, bustling fighter, rushing his opponent at every opportunity and showing great stamina and courage, even though he was floored briefly in the first round. The Italian was always dangerous but Eddie steadily built up his points lead. Eddie cut loose in the final round and floored Palermo again as he went all out for a decisive finish, but in the end he had to be content with the points decision.

In the weeks that followed the British Boxing Board of Control wrote to the New York State Athletic Commission and the National Boxing Association pushing Eddie's claims for a world title challenge in the event of Sugar Ray Robinson relinquishing his title, but the NBA had already agreed that Charlie Fusari and Johnny Bratton should box for the vacant title, even though Robinson still claimed to be Welterweight Champion, while George Gainsford, Robinson's manager, stated emphatically that Ray would defend his title against Eddie in July in London.

To add to the confusion, in April, the EBU ordered Eddie to defend his European title against the Frenchman Charles Humez. Boxing News considered the decision to go ahead with the contest against Humez as a high risk strategy given the possibility of a world title fight and the paper saw Humez as potentially the most dangerous opponent of Eddie's professional career to date.

Having beaten the Spanish Champion, Antonio Monzon on points in London in April, the match with Humez was set for Coney Beach Arena in Porthcawl on June 13th, and after four months as European Champion, Eddie lost his title to the tough, bustling Frenchman in front of a crowd of ten thousand stunned supporters. Humez boxed with confidence and gained in strength as the contest went on and Eddie was unable to make his customary impression with the left hand. Late in the contest Thomas desperately tried to increase the tempo, but at the end Humez was a comfortable points winner. The Frenchman was obviously elated but Eddie looked tired and was cut over both eyes and on his forehead. In contrast to Humez, he looked totally dejected as he realised that his world title opportunity had just slipped away.

Charles Humez, also known as the "Lion of Flanders" returned to Britain in June 1953 and challenged Randolph Turpin for the European Middleweight title but lost on points over fifteen rounds. The contest was recognised by the British Boxing Board of Control and the EBU as being for the world title but the Americans refused to recognise the match. In an attempt to regain the world championship, Turpin was subsequently matched with Carl (Bobo) Olson in New York and lost on points over the fifteen round course.

Eddie was back in action on July 24th, 1951 at Selhurst Park, the home of Crystal Palace AFC. Thomas won by a knockout in the fourth round flooring his opponent, Eric McQuade with a beautiful right cross. It is interesting to note that Eddie often had difficulty with his weight and came in at 10st 11lbs for this contest, with McQuade a couple of pounds heavier. Eddie was delighted with his win, which helped ease the disappointment of the Humez fight and in August he beat Giel de Roode again, this time on points over ten rounds in Bangor.

In October 1951, disaster struck once more when he lost his British and Empire titles to Wally Thom. They met at Harringay on October 16th with Thom emerging with a narrow victory on points over fifteen rounds, thus repeating an amateur decision over Eddie many years before on a show in North Wales.

Eddie was traditionally a slow starter and Thom took the early part of the contest with Eddie seemingly content to let the Birkenhead man do all the fighting while he relied on countering. Weight-making had once more been a problem for Eddie and he did not begin to exert real pressure until the eleventh round, by which time he was way behind on points. He was now winning rounds by a decisive margin and Eddie punished Thom severely during the last few rounds as he went all out for victory. Unfortunately, at the bell, the referee raised Thom's arm and Eddie could only stand there and watch as the Lonsdale Belt was clasped around Thom's waist. Eddie had never actually had the belt in his hands, but victory over Wally Thom would have given him outright possession of the most magnificent trophy in sport.

During his career, Eddie had trouble with his hands and often needed painkilling injections. He enjoyed playing football and cricket and this led to the need for a cartilage operation which kept him out of the ring for eighteen months. He was also engaged in a constant battle with the scales and even though he returned to the ring in April 1953, he was not the same boxer. He was unable to rediscover the momentum of the early part of his career, though he managed a draw in Belfast against Bunty Adamson in a British title eliminator. The contest took place at the King's Hall, a venue famous for its atmosphere on big fight night. During the 1940's and 50's World Flyweight Champion Rinty Monaghan boxed there many times, and curiously enough he always sang to the crowd after a win, his song being "When Irish Eyes Are Smiling". Eddie had to return to Belfast for the rematch in February, 1954 and this time he lost the decision over twelve rounds. When he was beaten on points over eight rounds in Manchester by Ron Duncombe on December 10th, 1954, he realised that the time had come to retire from boxing.

The end of his boxing career marked the beginning of an even more remarkable career as trainer, manager, promoter and cut-man of extraordinary repute, but his links with mining continued, with much of the money he earned in the ring being invested in small mines.

Eddie started a couple of gyms in local pubs. His first venture was at the Bush Hotel in Dowlais along with Johnny Harris, who is now in his eighties and is still involved in training youngsters at the Dowlais Amateur Boxing Club. He is also an active member of the Welsh Ex-Boxers' Association. They soon moved to the King's Head, located in South Street before moving into the gym in High Street, Penydarren, and the Dowlais Amateur Boxing Club saw the emergence of some extremely talented young boxers.

The high point came when Howard Winstone won a gold medal for Wales at the Empire Games held in Cardiff in 1958 but there were successes also for Gerald Jones, Don James, John Gamble and Malcolm Price. They accumulated titles galore and there were many international vests in what became one of Britain's most successful gyms.

After his success at the Empire Games, Howard turned to the professional ranks and the others gradually followed. As the partnership between Howard and Eddie became so successful, so too the achievements of the gym snowballed. Howard and the others were joined by Carl Gizzi from Rhyl, Eddie Avoth from Cardiff, Roger Tighe, a Commonwealth Games gold medallist at Lightheavyweight from Hull and Ken Buchanan from Scotland, already a boxer of immense talent.

The triumphs are almost too numerous to mention. Winstone and Buchanan were both steered to world title victories while Eddie Avoth became British and Commonwealth Lightheavyweight Champion. Carl Gizzi challenged Jack Bodell unsuccessfully for the British Heavyweight title while Roy John challenged Chris Finnegan for the titles he had taken from Eddie Avoth. During this time the reputation of Eddie and his stable was attracting boxers from all over the country. Middleweight Phil Matthews was trained in Merthyr and boxed Bunny Sterling for the British title. At the request of Jack Solomons, Eddie took Danny McAlinden to the British Heavyweight title having first worked his corner on the Ali/Frazier bill at Madison Square Garden in March 1971 when McAlinden beat Ali's brother Rahman on points over six rounds.

Irishman McAlinden was born in Newry but had lived in Coventry for many years. He was originally managed by George Middleton, the manager of Randolph Turpin, but when George became ill, Solomons took over the managerial reigns, and he brought Eddie in almost immediately.

When Danny was matched with Jack Bodell for the British Heavyweight Championship, he was determined to win quickly in what was Britain's first open-air show for many years, the venue being Villa Park in Birmingham. Bodell was floored twice in the first round though both men ended up on the floor. In the second round, Jack Bodell went to the floor three times and was counted out by referee George

Smith after just one minute and thirtyone seconds of the round. The contest had been wildly exciting while it lasted, but much of the credit for McAlinden's win should go to Eddie for the way he prepared Danny in Merthyr for his big night.

Eddie's brothers, Hughie and Ronnie often formed part of the corner team. Hughie had enjoyed success in both amateur and professional codes while Ronnie's experience was restricted to the amateur ranks. He boxed in the Welsh ABA Championships but was stopped when he sustained a cut eyebrow which required four stitches and this deprived him of his international vest. He had been chosen to represent Wales against Switzerland but had to withdraw from the team because of the eye injury and so, his opportunity was lost, but his experience was obviously valuable in the corner in later years. As a team they each had knowledge and experience and there was always a sense of calm with Eddie in charge.

As the years passed Eddie developed an enviable reputation as a cut man and his skills were often in demand. The story of how he saved Ken Buchanan's title against Ismael Laguna by nicking with a razor blade the base of the swelling which was closing Ken's eye is now the stuff of legend. Such was the esteem in which he was held, when Henry Cooper parted company with his long-time cut man Danny Holland, Eddie was called in to handle the corner and he did this for Cooper's last three championship fights, earning the praise of the British Boxing Board of Control's chief medical adviser Dr Adrian Whiteson in the process. Eddie was often asked what he used in the treatment of eye injuries and his replies often added to the mystique. He sometimes said that he used "duff", (coal waste) from Merthyr Vale Colliery and at other times claimed to have bought some magical potion from Dowlais market. In truth, ofcourse, he was only able to use the adrenalin solution permitted by the Board, together with vaseline and carefully applied pressure.

As the seventies ran their course Eddie became the manager of Colin Jones, the gravedigger from Gorseinon, and steered him to British, Commonwealth and European Welterweight titles, thus emulating his own achievements as a boxer. He also secured three world title fights for Colin, two against Milton McCrory for the WBC title and the other against Don Curry for the WBA version of the crown. The first contest with McCrory took place in Reno, Nevada in March, 1983 and ended in a draw. Their second contest took place in the furnace-like conditions of Las Vegas in August of the same year and Colin was adjudged to have lost on points over twelve rounds. Colin was now out of the picture as far as the WBC were concerned and after taking a couple of contests during 1984 to re-establish himself Frank Warren stepped in and brokered a deal for him to meet Don Curry at the NEC in Birmingham for the WBA title with the contest taking place on January 19th, 1985. Colin had barely got going when he sustained a gaping gash across the bridge of his nose and the referee was forced to intervene in the fourth round. This was a devastating defeat for Colin. He was in superb condition as always and was frustrated by the ending because he had so much still left in the tank. Sadly, the world title had eluded him and he opted for retirement, but after Colin retired, Eddie drifted from the scene leaving a huge void in Wales.

Eddie had been watching Colin as a young man, boxing out of the Penyrheol club and guided by his life-long friend, Gareth Bevan, who was always to be seen in Colin's corner throughout his career. Colin won the ABA Welterweight title in both 1976 and 1977 and was one of our youngest ever Olympic representatives at the Montreal Games in 1976 where he was eliminated by the Romanian, Victor Silberman.

Colin made an impressive start to his professional career showing great boxing skill together with immense power. On April 1st, 1980, he challenged Kirkland Laing for the British Welterweight title and conceded round after round to the talented champion. But Colin was gradually cutting down the ring, and in the ninth round, he finally caught up with Laing and stopped him with what were now his trademark shots. Colin went on to win the Lonsdale Belt outright, a feat which had eluded Eddie, and after winning both the Commonwealth and European crowns, Eddie was determined that Colin should have his world title opportunities, which sadly, he himself did not get during his own career.

When Eddie started out as a manager it was not possible to hold a promoter's licence at the same time and he overcame the problem by persuading his friend Billy Long to take out a licence. Their first promotion was at the Miners' Hall in Merthyr Tydfil on December 19th, 1961 when Johnny Gamble topped the bill against Joe Somerville. Billy was subsequently followed by Eddie's brother Cyril as promoter. Cyril had enjoyed success as an amateur boxer and had himself boxed for Wales and the arrangement allowed Eddie to guarantee work for his successful stable. His boxers worked for Jack Solomons and Harry Levene, two intense promotional rivals and he also worked closely with Les Roberts, matchmaker at the National Sporting Club in London's Piccadilly. Eddie steadfastly refused to align himself with one promoter or promotional group and this principled approach obviously cost him a great deal of money. He also had a disagreement with Mike Barrett and Mickey Duff following Howard Winstone's world title win over Mitsunori Seki and this denied his boxers access to major London promotions for a few years. Eddie invested heavily in shows in Wales and for many years he was the one man who kept boxing alive in the principality.

Eventually the Board's regulations were changed and this enabled Eddie to take out his own promoter's licence and he staged some memorable battles. He promoted the contests between Merthyr's Les Pickett and Alan Richardson, one of which was for the British Featherweight title and the other an eliminator. These were tough, uncompromising battles, and at the second Scots Boxing Hall of Fame induction weekend held in Glasgow in October, 2004 I met Alan Richardson and talked to him at length. He was full of praise for Les Pickett and named him as his toughest opponent. Alan admitted that the closest he ever came to showing the white flag in the ring was against Pickett and but for the encouraging words of his manager Trevor Callighan he would have turned his back on Les. Such is the fine line between victory and defeat in the boxing ring.

Eddie also staged the contests between Merthyr boys Johnny Wall and Martyn Galleozzie, both epic battles for the Welsh Lightweight title. Johnny lost his title in the first encounter but regained it in the return at the Rhydycar Leisure Centre in Merthyr in what turned out to be one of the best fights of 1977.

In the late seventies Eddie struck up a partnership with John Conteh, the former WBC World Lightheavyweight Champion. John had been due to defend his title against Miguel Cuello in Monte Carlo. Promotional difficulties and a disagreement with the British Boxing Board of Control resulted in Conteh's withdrawal days before the contest and he was stripped of his title by the WBC. Various promoters attempted to align themselves with Conteh but it was Eddie who staged his next contest with the Texan Joe Cokes on February 7th, 1978. Joe was the brother of former World Welterweight Champion Curtis Cokes, who held the title from 1966 until he was beaten by Jose Napoles. At the time, John had been out of the ring for almost a year and he was taken the full ten rounds by Cokes at the Sobell Centre in Islington, North London.

Eddie then worked briefly in association with Frank Warren but I think his finest promotion came at the Eisteddfod Pavilion in Gowerton in August 1980 when Colin Jones defended his British Welterweight title against Peter Neal. The atmosphere was magnificent and Eddie, showing the Jack Solomons touch, engaged the Dowlais Male Choir to sing at the event and I shall never forget the thrill of conducting the Welsh National Anthem before the contest began.

When the British Boxing Board of Control celebrated its fiftieth anniversary in 1979 Eddie Thomas was honoured at the banquet at Cardiff's City Hall as the man who had contributed most to Welsh boxing over the previous half century. His achievements towered above all others.

As the years passed he received a variety of honours. He was inducted into the Welsh Sports Hall of Fame, and he was honoured by the Boxing Writers' Club, an honour that was important to him because it came from within the sport. He was awarded the Freedom of Merthyr as well as an MBE. For a time he was a member of the Broadcasting Council for Wales and finally, he became Mayor of his beloved Merthyr Tydfil, the town which he always talked of with such knowledge and passion. This, for him, was the honour which topped all the others.

He was immensely proud of his home town and spoke eloquently of its industrial, cultural and sporting heritage. He loved the people of Merthyr and they too, loved him and he never wanted to leave the town. Even though he made and lost large sums of money in his mining ventures he always provided cheap coal for pensioners and did a great deal of charity work. His love of soccer shone through in his generous support of Merthyr Tydfil AFC over many years. He cared about so many aspects of community life and never missed an opportunity of raising the profile of the town. In truth, Merthyr could not have wished for a finer ambassador.

Eddie Thomas died on June 2nd, 1997 after a long battle against cancer. His funeral at Tabernacle Chapel, Merthyr Tydfil was an unforgettable experience. The singing would have pleased him, especially the old Welsh funeral favourite "O fryniau Caersalem" and later at the crematorium "Bless This House", the song he first sang to the crowd at Harringay all those years ago. Ultimately, the service was a celebration of the life of a great man, and rarely have so many people been reduced to tears of laughter as we listened to speaker after speaker share their memories of Eddie, a true champion and maker of champions.

During the service, the Rev David Protheroe expressed the view that a statue should be erected in memory of Eddie and an appeal fund was launched immediately. There was much debate about where the statue should be placed and it was eventually decided that it should be situated at the Bethesda Memorial Gardens, the site of the long-demolished Bethesda Chapel, the chapel attended by the town's best known composer, Dr Joseph Parry, and only a short distance from the composer's birthplace at Chapel Row.

For Eddie, with his love of Merthyr and its traditions there could not have been a more appropriate position for his memorial. Parry was often referred to as the "Bachgen bach o Ferthyr", the little boy from Merthyr. The plaque beneath Eddie's statue refers to the "Bachgen bach o Colliers' Row", the little boy from Colliers' Row, but his achievements transcend boxing and mark him out as one of the great Welshmen of the twentieth century.

Eddie Thomas

Born in Merthyr Tydfil, July 27th, 1926
Welsh ABA Lightweight Champion 1946
ABA Lightweight Champion 1946
Welsh International and Great Britain Representative

Professional Titles:
Welsh Welterweight Champion
British, Empire and European Welterweight Champion

Professional Record

1946
Jun 4th	Ivor Simpson	w.pts.4	London
Jul 20th	Reg Quinlan	w.pts.6	Aberdare
Aug 28th	Don Chiswell	w.rsf.3	Merthyr
Sep 4th	Bob Ramsey	w.pts.6	Cardiff
Nov 5th	Dick Shields	w.pts.6	London
Dec 6th	Ginger Ward	w.pts.6	Trealaw

1947
Feb 20th	Jimmy Brunt	w.ko.6	Cwmbran
Mar 18th	Billy Walker	w.rsf.4	London
Apr 18th	Bill Cadby	w.pts.8	Merthyr
Jun 16th	Jean Wanes	w.pts.8	Newport
Sep 8th	Yrjoe Pituliainen	l.rsf.3	London
Nov 3rd	Kid Marcel	w.rtd.4	London
Dec 9th	Willy Wimms	w.rtd.3	London

1948
Jan 26th	Henry Hall	w.pts.8	London
Mar 16th	Gwyn Williams	l.pts.10	London
(British welterweight title eliminator)			
May 31st	Jack Phillips	w.pts.10	London
(Welsh welterweight title eliminator)			
Jun 23rd	Chris Adcock	w.rsf.3	Cheltenham
Jul 26th	Ernie Roderick	w.pts.8	London
Sep 21st	Gwyn Williams	w.pts.12	London
(Welsh Welterweight Title)			
Nov 17th	Willie Whyte	w.ko.6	Abergavenny
Dec 6th	Giel de Roode	w.rtd.7	London

1949
Jan 10th	Billy Exley	w.pts.10	Newcastle
Feb 7th	Billy Graham	w.pts.10	London
Jun 9th	Stan Hawthorne	w.rsf.3	Liverpool
(British welterweight title eliminator)			
Jun 27th	Job Roos	w.pts.10	Abergavenny
Sep 6th	Ernie Roderick	w.pts:12	London
(British welterweight title eliminator)			
Nov 15th	Henry Hall	w.pts.15	London
(British Welterweight Title)			

1950
Jan 16th	Constant Reypens	w.pts.10	Abergavenny
Apr 25th	Bruno Marostegan	w.pts.10	London
May 22nd	Emile Delmine	w.rsf.6	Abergavenny
Jun 21st	Henri Hecquard	w.pts.10	Porthcawl
Jul 19th	Gilbert Ussin	w.pts.10	Porthcawl
Sep 13th	Cliff Curvis	w.pts.15	Swansea
Nov 14th	Titi Clavel	d.8	London

1951
Jan 27th	Pat Patrick	w.ko.13	Johannesburg
(British Empire Welterweight Title)			
Feb 19th	Michele Palermo	w.pts.15	Carmarthen
(European Welterweight Title)			
Apr 24th	Antonio Monzon	w.pts.10	London
Jun 13th	Charles Humez	l.pts.15	Porthcawl
Jul 24th	Eric McQuade	w.ko.4	Selhurst Park
Aug 30th	Giel de Roode	w.pts.10	Bangor
Oct 16th	Wally Thom	l.pts.15	London
(British and Empire Welterweight Titles)			

1952
Inactive

1953
Apr 27th	George Roe	w.pts.8	Cardiff
Jun 1st	Kit Pompey	w.pts.10	Newport
Jul 27th	Roy Baird	w.rsf.7	Cardiff
Sep 25th	Bunty Adamson	d.12	Belfast
(British title eliminator)			

1954
Feb 27th	Bunty Adamson	l.pts.12	Belfast
(British title eliminator)			
Jul 19th	Terry Ratcliffe	w.pts.8	Cardiff
Dec 10th	Ron Duncombe	l.pts.8	Manchester

Eddie pictured with "Dolly" the horse (courtesy of the Daily Express)

EDDIES BROTHERS - THE FIGHTING THOMASES

  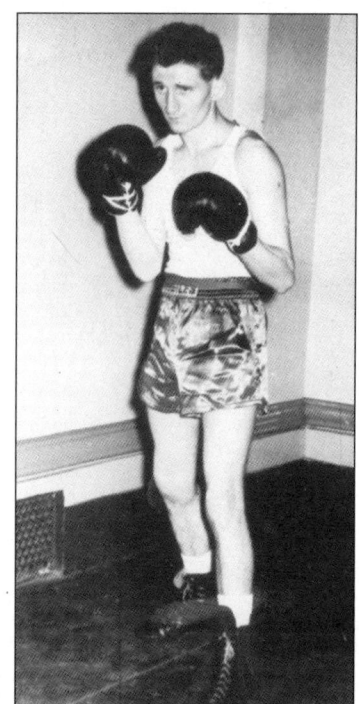

Hughie   *Ronnie*   *Cyril*

Eddie Thomas (left) pictured with promoter Jack Solomons (courtesy of the Daily Express)

Eddie Thomas sings to the crowd after beating Henry Hall. (courtesy of the Western Mail)

Colin Jones. British, Commonwealth and European Welterweight Champion. The last of Eddie's Champions

2

Howard Winstone

Howard Winstone was born in Merthyr Tydfil on April 15th, 1939 and as a young boy growing up in the town he was drawn to the sport of boxing. As an amateur Howard was trained initially by Billy Evans before eventually teaming up with Eddie Thomas, but before achieving his goal, Howard had to overcome a handicap which would undoubtedly have shattered lesser men. While working at a local toy factory he lost the tops of three fingers on his right hand in an accident with a metal press, but for a young man with his spirit and determination, he was, remarkably, only out of the ring for a year.

He was ready to return to boxing in 1956 and he joined the stable of Eddie Thomas, just a few yards from his Penydarren home and because of the severity of his injury, he was transformed from a fighter into a supremely skilled boxer. In less than eighteen months he won the Welsh ABA Bantamweight title, the ABA Bantamweight title and he was to become the only boxer in England and Wales to capture a gold medal at the 1958 Empire Games, held appropriately in Cardiff. Added to this impressive catalogue of achievements he also boxed for Wales.

As the first star of Dowlais Amateur Boxing Club it was fitting that he should turn professional with Eddie Thomas in what became an extremely successful partnership. He made his professional debut at Wembley on February 24th, 1959 when he beat Billy Graydon on points over six rounds. This was a high profile bill with Joe Erskine topping against the American Willie Pastrano, who was given a boxing lesson by the Cardiff man. Contests followed for Howard in Newport, Cardiff, Porthcawl, Aberdare and Ebbw Vale. On September 1st, he beat Billy Calvert in the seventh round at the Ynys at Aberdare on a show promoted by Merthyr promoter Theo Davies. Calvert would appear twice more in the opposite corner during Howard's career.

From his earliest contests Howard made a huge impression and it was clear that Winstone possessed one of the finest left-hands ever seen in a British ring, frequently throwing four or five in succession. His footwork was dazzling and he could turn his opponent so quickly on the ropes. As soon as he felt the ropes on his back, he would move away from a potentially dangerous situation at lightning speed and his opponents were left punching thin air. This had to be seen to be believed and it unquestionably rattled many of his opponents. I remember the night of August 2nd, 1962 when the Ghanaian Dennis Adjei desperately chased after his elusive opponent, only to find that Winstone had moved on. It was the same on the night of April 29th,

1963 when Howard returned to Sophia Gardens, Cardiff to face the former European Champion Gracieux Lamperti. Howard totally outclassed the vastly more experienced Frenchman and fully lived up to his description as the Welsh Wizard.

Howard was undefeated after twentyfour contests when he challenged Terry Spinks for the British Featherweight title. The contest took place on May 2nd, 1961 at Wembley and it was billed as the battle of the Golden Boys for a purse of £12,055. Terry Spinks had won the gold medal at the Melbourne Olympics in 1956 while Howard had of course captured the Empire Games gold. The posters for the contest, together with the handbills and the programmes were all printed following the "Golden" theme and indeed, it turned out to be a golden night for Welsh boxing. Thousands of Welshmen went up to Wembley for the fight and they were rewarded with a sparkling Winstone performance. Spinks retired after ten rounds and the arena became a cauldron of ecstatic celebration as the Lonsdale Belt was strapped around Howard's waist. The fight was handled by Welsh referee Ike Powell, who had been called in as a late replacement, but his job was made easier by the decisiveness of Winstone's performance.

Outright possession of the Lonsdale Belt had eluded Eddie Thomas and he was determined that the same thing should not happen to Howard. In April, 1962, Howard retained his title at Wembley stopping Derry Treanor in the fourteenth round and on May 30th, just over a year after winning the title, he made the belt his own property by forcing Cardiff puncher Harry Carroll to retire in six rounds at Maindy Stadium.

On July 9th, 1963 he won the European title beating Alberto Serti of Italy when the referee stopped the contest in the fourteenth round, the contest again being staged at Maindy Stadium with local bookmaker Stan Cottle involved in the promotion. This was one of the few contests where there were no photographs available and this was because of a newspaper photographers' strike. It was a busy year for Howard during which he made three successful defences of his British title and became the proud owner of a second Lonsdale Belt. Following wins over Johnny Morrissey at the Kelvin Hall in Glasgow and Billy Calvert at Porthcawl, Howard secured his second belt in what was then record time by beating another Scot, John O'Brien at the National Sporting Club in London on December 9th.

The National Sporting Club played a vital part in the development of regulated boxing as we know it today. The old NSC opened at 43, King Street, Covent Garden on March 5th, 1891 and was founded by A.F. "Peggy" Bettinson and John Fleming with Lord Lonsdale as the first president. It was he who donated the first National Sporting Club Challenge Belts and this was to prove crucial in the regulating of championship contests. The belts took the name of Lord Lonsdale when the British Boxing Board of Control came into being in 1929.

Jim Driscoll, Freddie Welsh, Tom Thomas and Jimmy Wilde became extremely popular with members of the NSC but the growth of boxing through the 1920's created difficulties for the "Club". Basically, it was too small and a larger venue was needed.

The artist W. Howard Robinson produced a superb painting of the contest between Jim Driscoll and Joe Bowker at the NSC which now hangs in the offices of the British Boxing Board of Control while one of Robinson's later pieces features the contest between Jimmy Wilde and the Irish-American Joe Lynch which took place at the Club in 1919. The title of this picture is "A Welsh Victory at the National Sporting Club". During the 1960's there were many Welsh victories at the NSC, notably by members of Eddie's stable and it is appropriate from a historical perspective that Howard Winstone should have followed in the footsteps of his illustrious Welsh predecessors by defending his title there.

By now, the Club, after several relocations, was based at the Café Royal in Regent Street and was headed by Charles Forte and John Harding. There was no real connection with the old NSC but attempts were made to uphold the exclusivity and traditions of the old Club where silence was observed during rounds. Unfortunately, a limited budget meant that it was now virtually impossible to stage championship contests at the Club, but almost to a man, the stable of the 60's upheld the traditions of this remarkable institution.

Howard's only loss to date had come at the hands of the little known American, Leroy Jeffery at Leeds Town Hall on November 5th, 1962 when he was dramatically stopped in the second round. The effect of this defeat could have been detrimental, but in one of boxing's ironies it is interesting to note that just three weeks later, Jeffery lost on points to Sheffield's Billy Calvert over ten rounds in Manchester. Billy was one of the leading featherweights of the time but during his career, he was beaten three times by Howard. In Winstone's contest with Jeffery, the action of Eddie Thomas in grabbing hold of Howard's ankle, thus preventing him from rising after a knockdown, may have been a hugely decisive moment in Howard's career, for, just two years later his skills were being hailed by no less a figure than Angelo Dundee, the trainer of Muhammad Ali, when Howard comprehensively beat Baby Luis, one of Dundee's Cuban protégés at Wembley.

The contest with Luis took place on December 1st, 1964, but it had already been a busy year. On January 28th Howard was adjudged by referee Jack Hart to have lost on points over ten rounds to the American Don Johnson, but in his next contest he beat the tough Nigerian Rafiu King on points over ten rounds, again at Wembley. King was an exceptional fighter and was a noted puncher and Howard once admitted to me that King was the hardest puncher he ever faced, but the superior skills of Winstone prevailed in this encounter. In May he was back in the same Wembley ring forcing the Italian Lino Mastellaro to retire in eight rounds in a European title defence, and so the momentum continued.

His first contest in 1965 saw him travel to Rome where he beat the Frenchman Yves Desmarets in yet another defence of his European title and he followed this by gaining revenge over Don Johnson with a points win over ten rounds at Carmarthen. After wins over Lalo Guerrero and Jose Legra he was finally given the opportunity he so richly deserved. In 1964, promoter Jack Solomons had virtually secured a contest with Sugar Ramos for the world title, but this eventually went to Vicente Saldivar, who forced Ramos to retire in eleven rounds in Mexico City, but now, at last, under the promotional banner of Harry Levene, Howard got his big chance.

On September 7th, 1965 Howard was matched with Vicente Saldivar at London's Earls Court Arena. This was a great night for Welshmen and a great night for Winstone and from my seat it seemed that Howard was a points winner after an epic battle, but London referee Bill Williams was of the opinion that the tough Mexican had done enough to win. In the early rounds Winstone built up a massive points lead with his superior left hand work but the tough little man who had been likened to a pocket Marciano then began to whittle down the lead and came away with the crucial decision.

The contest had been eagerly awaited in Merthyr Tydfil and particularly in the little village of Cefn Coed, where Howard now lived. Eddie had arranged public workouts at the local Community Centre and these caused great excitement when well respected London journalists began to arrive. People such as George Whiting, Sam Leitch, Reg Gutteridge, Alan Hoby, Desmond Hackett and many others turned out to see Howard being put through his paces and I remember walking out with Howard after one of these sessions. It was clear that his biggest fear was that he should not let his supporters down. Thousands of fans would be making the trip to London and Howard valued their support so much.

He did not let anyone down, but we were all disappointed by the result. The people of Merthyr turned out in their thousands to welcome him home at the Town Hall and this became something of a ritual.

Howard engaged in two further battles with Saldivar, one at Cardiff, and the other in Mexico City, the latter being a tough battle in which Winstone was stopped in twelve rounds in a last desperate effort by Saldivar. Howard later spoke about the effects of boxing at altitude and its effect on his legs, and this, coupled with the formidable task of facing Saldivar on home territory, the Aztec Stadium, was just too much to ask. Just how close Howard came to breaking the will of Saldivar we shall never know. It is said that if Howard had been able to survive that fateful twelfth round he would have won the title because Saldivar was exhausted, but Eddie Thomas was not prepared to risk injury and threw in the towel, much to Howard's disgust at the time. The battle had taken so much out of the champion that Saldivar immediately announced his retirement from boxing.

Winstone and Saldivar had taken each other almost to the limits of their very being, and their names will be forever linked in the way we think of Muhammad Ali and Joe Frazier after the "Thriller in Manila", where Eddie Futch did much the same for Joe as Eddie had done for Howard. Similarly, their contests rank alongside those between Willie Pep and Sandy Saddler as part of boxing folklore.

Howard Winstone finally won the world title when he was matched against Mitsunori Seki of Japan at London's Royal Albert Hall on January 23rd, 1968, the title having fallen vacant on the champion's retirement. Winstone and Seki provided the natural pairing since both had been beaten by Saldivar. Howard stopped Seki in the ninth round when Seki sustained a nasty cut above the left eye. Referee Roland Dakin, officiating in his first world title fight, took Seki to his corner to inspect the injury and stopped the contest, but Howard may even have knocked his man out had the fight been allowed to continue for another two rounds. He was systematically grinding his opponent down. Even so, it was generally acknowledged that Howard was now past his best and his domestic life was beset with problems, and it was, in truth, a miracle that he was able to perform as well as he did, but such were his standards that he still had the skill, determination and courage to achieve his ultimate goal. During the contest Howard paced himself admirably and a certain loss of speed seemed to be replaced with rather more solid punching. He was planting his feet a little more than usual, and Seki took a great deal of punishment to the body.

Howard was now Featherweight Champion of the World and became the third Welsh "W" in the record books alongside Freddie Welsh and Jimmy Wilde and there was a lovely moment at the end of the contest when Vicente Saldivar was on hand to present Howard with the World Championship trophy, almost as though he were giving the new champion his seal of approval.

Howard had been having difficulty with his weight for some time and he looked drawn when I saw him at Coney Beach Arena, Porthcawl on the night before he was due to defend his title for the first time. Sadly, the title had come too late in his career to ensure financial reward and unfortunately, Howard was stopped in five rounds by the Cuban, Jose Legra. His left eye was badly damaged by a looping punch in the first round and the eye closed immediately. The arena was overtaken by an eerie silence and it was clear to us all that one of our greatest boxers ever had no chance of retaining the title he had chased for so long. Referee Harry Gibbs gave Howard every opportunity but in the end was left with no option but to stop the contest. This turned out to be Howard's last fight, though he did not announce his retirement as such, but relinquished his British title in February 1969.

I have no doubt in my mind that Howard's finest contest took place at Ninian Park, Cardiff on June 15th, 1967 when he met Vicente Saldivar for the second time for the Featherweight Championship of the World. Never was a man greater in defeat.

The contest took place before a crowd of something like 30,000 people on a hot summer night and there must have been only one man in the ground that felt Saldivar had won. That man was referee Wally Thom who scored the contest $73^{3/4}$ points to $73^{3/4}$ in favour of the Mexican.

Thom was not the ideal choice for this contest since he had taken away the British and Empire Welterweight titles from Eddie Thomas and had deprived him of outright ownership of the Lonsdale Belt and it was known that they were not the best of friends. It is also worth noting at this point that as I was completing scoring tests at Leeds Town Hall a few years later in the quest for my own referee's licence, cornermen were most apprehensive to see Thom in charge of their boxers and I was concerned at this lack of confidence in his ability. The whole issue centred on inconsistency which is a rather worrying quality in any referee.

Eddie Thomas was furious at the decision in Saldivar's favour, and though he rarely swore in public, he addressed the secretary of the British Boxing Board of Control in these terms: "I hope you are proud of your bloody British justice tonight", while Howard in the weeks and months ahead would question his treatment that night, totally bewildered by the experience. He felt badly let down and could not understand why he had not been given the decision.

The words of the highly respected sports writer Peter Wilson will live in my mind along with my memories of the actual contest. He wrote in the Daily Mirror: "And so it all came to nothing. The sound and the fury, the skill and the courage, and I care not what anyone else says. I shall remember June 15th, 1967, as the night when Howard Winstone won the Featherweight Championship of the World at Ninian Park, Cardiff. In my opinion, he was robbed of his just desserts".

When the fight began, it was almost a carbon copy of their first encounter. Winstone was dictating the early rounds with that immaculate left hand of his. The atmosphere was even more emotionally intense than for the first battle since we were home soil and the air was filled with song, noise and an overwhelming measure of Welsh "hwyl".

Winstone was completely outboxing Saldivar as the champion tried to bring Howard within reach of his relentlessly moving arms. By the ninth round Howard was well ahead on points, but as in their first contest, it was roughly from this point that the Welshman began to weaken , though Saldivar already looked a beaten man and his efforts took on an air of desperation, with both his eyes marked.

It is undeniable that Winstone came perilously close to defeat in a traumatic fourteenth round which saw his manager Eddie Thomas perched on the ring apron yelling advice to a man who was on his feet, but fighting on sheer instinct. Somehow, Howard showed a remarkable will to survive. It was no disgrace that he went to the floor under sustained pressure, but the fact that he knelt at six and rose to go straight back at Saldivar spoke volumes for his courage.

The last round went almost beyond the bounds of realism. Saldivar launched a furious attack but Winstone boxed with all his defensive skill and at times took the fight to the champion. In doing so he must have made it an even round, but alas, when the bell rang, the referee raised Saldivar's arm. Once the referee's decision has been given, arguments are academic, but in later years Saldivar acknowledged Howard's superiority in their Cardiff battle which undoubtedly saw the Merthyr man at his peak.

Howard Winstone engaged in sixtyseven contests during his career. He won sixtyone of those contests and lost six, with three of those defeats coming at the hands of Vicente Saldivar. He was without equal in Britain and Europe during this time and defeated all his nominated challengers. There were quality fighters in the division and there were intense rivalries such as that between Lennie "The Lion" Williams from Maesteg and Frankie "The Tiger" Taylor from Lancaster. They met on two occasions with Taylor as the winner but unfortunately, his career was curtailed by injury and Williams was the one who eventually challenged for the title. Lennie was a dangerous puncher but Howard emphasised his superiority stopping him in the eighth round at Aberavon and gaining the first notch on a third Lonsdale Belt, which he would surely have made his own had he decided to continue boxing.

Howard's record stands up to the closest scrutiny with his wins over Don Johnson, Rafiu King and Jose Legra bearing testimony to true world class and without the rivalry of a fighter such as Vicente Saldivar, he may have enjoyed a much longer reign as world champion, but these were career defining fights, the like of which many boxers crave and his place in boxing history is secure.

When his career was over, life was less than kind to Howard and there were business failures which drained his financial resources, but there were honours galore. While at his peak he was a three-time winner of the "Western Mail" Sports Personality of the Year. He was awarded the MBE, the Freedom of his beloved Merthyr Tydfil and in 1996 he was inducted into the Welsh Sports Hall of Fame.

He was invited to boxing functions all over the country and was involved with the Welsh Ex-Boxers' Association, carrying off the office of President with his own brand of humour, not to mention great dignity. He was extremely popular whenever he was introduced from the ring on fight night and the biggest cheer always seemed to be reserved for him.

He loved his family and enjoyed his continued involvement in the sport. He visited Canastota to witness the posthumous induction of his old rival and great friend Vicente Saldivar into the International Boxing Hall of Fame, but little did we know that Howard would succumb so soon to his own health problems and in the early hours of Saturday, September 30th, 2000 Howard passed away at the tragically early age of sixtyone leaving everyone who knew him with a treasure trove of memories of the man they called the Welsh Wizard.

A week later, on Saturday, October 7th we gathered at St Tydfil's Parish Church in Merthyr for his funeral. It was an emotional day with Merthyr typically cloaked in grey and autumnal dampness in the air.

I arrived at the church well over an hour before the start of the service and all the seats were already taken. Looking around the church was like being in the ultimate "Hall of Fame". Barry John was one of the early arrivals from the world of rugby and then came Gareth Edwards, the other half of that immortal partnership, while the boxing world turned out in force, as expected.

It was heartwarming to see Ken Buchanan in attendance. Recently inducted into the International Boxing Hall of Fame in Canastota, New York, the former Lightweight Champion of the World had last trained in Merthyr over thirty years previously and the memories of his sparring sessions with Howard sprang immediately to mind. Dai Dower, Eddie Avoth, Cliff Curvis, Colin Jones and Alan Rudkin, champions all, were there together with more recent champions Steve Robinson and Robbie Regan. Later Alan Minter and Terry Downes, both middleweight champions of the world arrived to pay their respects.

Journalists John Lloyd, Ken Jones and Gareth Jones were present, friends of Howard and Eddie who had written at length on their respective achievements down the years. Champions, challengers, former opponents, friends and fans all gathered to pay their final tribute.

The service was conducted by the Rev David Protheroe and opened with the singing of "How Great Thou Art" which had the typical resonance of a predominantly male congregation. Moving tributes followed from local businessman and Freeman of Merthyr Stan Thomas, Don James, lifelong friend and Secretary of the Welsh Ex-Boxers' Association and Lord Brooks of Tremorfa representing the British Boxing Board of Control. Each, in his own way made a significant contribution and each had his own special memories of Howard.

Towards the end of the service there was an emotional moment when Ken Buchanan stepped forward and draped his tartan scarf over the coffin.

At the close, the congregation joined in the singing of "Cwm Rhondda", one of the great Welsh hymns and this was followed by "Mae Hen Wlad fy Nhadau", the Welsh National Anthem. Howard's body was then taken from the church to the strains of "The Boxer" by Simon and Garfunkel.

Huge crowds had gathered outside the church and had heard the service relayed on loudspeakers and now they watched in silence as the cortege left on its final journey through Merthyr, past the statue of mentor Eddie Thomas, up through Penydarren along the road of the long demolished gym and eventually to Cefn Coed cemetery.

There, at a spot not far from where Howard once lived, he was laid to rest to the sound of the Dowlais Male Choir, the choir I directed for almost twelve years, singing Morte Christe and Howard's favourite, Myfanwy, a piece composed by another of Merthyr's finest sons, Dr Joseph Parry.

The service ended with another rendition of the Welsh National Anthem, perhaps lacking the fervour with which we sang it on Howard's great nights but nevertheless a fitting tribute to our hero.

As I stepped forward to pay my own silent tribute at the graveside I stood next to a heartbroken Ken Buchanan. Memories of the great times came flooding back. I thought of the impeccable ring artist whose skills were without equal in Britain and Europe, the fun of just being in his company, the courage and sportsmanship and the sheer warmth of this most unassuming of men. And lastly, I thought of Howard's singing, for he loved to sing. He needed little persuasion to offer "Hello Dolly" and the Buddy Holly favourite "I Guess It Doesn't Matter Any More".

During the service Don James had expressed the view that a statue should be erected in Merthyr in Howard's memory. Don became the key figure in the launch of the appeal fund and worked tirelessly on fundraising events to ensure that the project became a reality, and exactly a year later, the statue was unveiled in the Merthyr Tydfil shopping precinct. And so, Howard now sits there watching over the people he loved so much. He loved the town, much as did Eddie, and it is difficult to imagine either of them living anywhere else.

Howard had touched the lives of so many people and I am not sure that he fully understood what he meant to us. Maybe had he been able to analyse the nature of that relationship, he would have ceased to be special.

Howard Winstone

Welsh ABA Bantamweight Champion 1958
ABA Bantamweight Champion 1958
Gold Medal at Bantamweight, Empire Games, Cardiff, 1958
Welsh International
British and European Featherweight Champion
World Featherweight Champion, 1968

Professional Record

1959
Date	Opponent	Result	Venue
Feb 24th	Billy Graydon	w.pts.6	Wembley
Mar 14th	Peter Sexton	w.pts.6	Newport
Apr 15th	Tommy Williams	w.pts.6	Cardiff
May 27th	Jackie Bowers	w.pts.6	Cardiff
Jun 24th	Jake O'Neale	w.pts.6	Porthcawl
Jul 14th	Ollie Wyllie	w.pts.6	Aberdare
Aug 8th	Hugh O'Neill	w.pts.8	Ebbw Vale
Sep 1st	Billy Calvert	w.rsf.7	Aberdare
Sep 14th	Joe Taylor	w.rsf.4	Ebbw Vale
Dec 14th	Billy Calvert	w.pts.8	London

1960
Date	Opponent	Result	Venue
Jan 14th	George O'Neill	w.rtd.7	Cardiff
Jan 25th	Robbie Wilson	w.pts.8	London
Feb 4th	Colin Salcombe	w.rsf.6	Birmingham
Feb 24th	Terry Rees	w.rsf.8	Cardiff
Mar 31st	Gordon Blakey	w.rtd.8	Cardiff
May 9th	George Carroll	w.rsf.4	Swansea
May 19th	Con Mount Bassie	w.pts.10	Birmingham
Jun 23rd	Noel Hazard	w.rsf.3	Birmingham
Jul 27th	Phil Jones	w.pts.10	Porthcawl
Aug 15th	Sergio Milan	w.rsf.6	Aberdare
Sep 22nd	Jean Renard	w.rsf.8	Cardiff
Oct 25th	Jean Renard	w.pts.8	Wembley
Nov 23rd	Roy Jacobs	w.pts.10	Carmarthen

1961
Date	Opponent	Result	Venue
Jan 19th	Floyd Robertson	w.pts.10	Cardiff
May 2nd	Terry Spinks	w.rtd.10	Wembley
	(British Featherweight Title)		
Aug 24th	Aryee Jackson	w.pts.10	Liverpool
Sep 4th	Gene Fossmire	w.pts.10	Cardiff
Nov 20th	Olli Maki	w.pts.10	Nottingham

1962
Date	Opponent	Result	Venue
Jan 9th	Dos Santos	w.pts.8	London
Apr 10th	Derry Treanor	w.rsf.14	Wembley
	(British Featherweight Title)		
May 30th	Harry Carroll	w.rtd.6	Cardiff
	(British Featherweight Title)		
Aug 2nd	Dennis Adjei	w.pts.8	Cardiff
Aug 18th	George Bowes	w.pts.10	Newtown
Sep 11th	Billy Davis	w.rsf.7	Wembley
Nov 5th	Leroy Jeffery	l.rsf.2	Leeds
Dec 10th	Freddie Dobson	w.rsf.3	Manchester
Dec 27th	Teddy Rand	w.rsf..3	London

1963
Date	Opponent	Result	Venue
Jan 31st	Johnny Morrissey	w.rsf.11	Glasgow
	(British Featherweight Title)		
Apr 29th	Gracieux Lamperti	w.rsf.8	Cardiff

1963 cont
Date	Opponent	Result	Venue
May 13th	Juan Cardenas	w.pts.8	London
Jul 9th	Alberto Serti	w.rsf.14	Cardiff
	(European Featherweight Title)		
Aug 20th	Billy Calvert	w.pts.15	Porthcawl
	(British and European Featherweight Titles)		
Sep 20th	Miguel Kimbo	w.pts.10	Corwen
Dec 9th	John O'Brien	w.pts.15	London
	(British and European Featherweight Titles)		

1964
Date	Opponent	Result	Venue
Jan 28th	Don Johnson	l.pts.10	London
Mar 24th	Rafiu King	w.pts.10	Wembley
May 12th	Lino Mastellaro	w.rtd.8	Wembley
	(European Featherweight Title)		
Jun 22nd	Phil Lundgren	w.rtd.7	London
Sep 21st	Jose Bisbal	w.pts.10	Manchester
Dec 1st	Baby Luis	w.pts.10	Wembley
Dec 14th	Boualem Belouard	w.pts.10	Nottingham

1965
Date	Opponent	Result	Venue
Jan 22nd	Yves Desmarets	w.pts.15	Rome
	(European Featherweight Title)		
Mar 29th	Don Johnson	w.pts.10	Carmarthen
Jun 1st	Lalo Guerrero	w.rsf.5	Wembley
Jun 22nd	Jose Legra	w.pts.10	Blackpool
Sep 7th	Vicente Saldivar	l.pts.15	London
	(World Featherweight Title)		
Dec 13th	Brian Cartwright	w.rsf.9	London

1966
Date	Opponent	Result	Venue
Mar 7th	Andrea Silanos	w.rsf.15	Sassari
	(European Featherweight Title)		
Sep 6th	Jean de Keers	w.rsf.3	London
	(European Featherweight Title)		
Oct 10th	Don Johnson	w.dis.4	Manchester
Dec 7th	Lennie Williams	w.rsf.8	Aberavon
	(British and European Featherweight Titles)		

1967
Date	Opponent	Result	Venue
Jan 17th	Richie Sue	w.pts.10	London
Jun 15th	Vicente Saldivar	l.pts.15	Cardiff
	(World Featherweight Title)		
Oct 14th	Vicente Saldivar	l.rtd.12	Mexico City
	(World Featherweight Title)		

1968
Date	Opponent	Result	Venue
Jan 23rd	Mitsunori Seki	w.rsf.9	London
	(Vacant World Featherweight Title)		
Apr 9th	Jimmy Anderson	w.pts.10	Wembley
Jul 24th	Jose Legra	l.rsf.5	Porthcawl
	(World Featherweight Title)		

Howard Winstone: British, European & World Featherweight Champion

3

Eddie Avoth

Eddie Avoth was born in Cardiff on May 2nd, 1945. He enjoyed a successful amateur career, winning several schoolboy and junior titles while boxing out of the famous Victoria Park Amateur Boxing Club. He represented Wales and won the Welsh Lightmiddleweight title in 1963. He then turned professional with Merthyr manager Eddie Thomas and in the early part of his career showed tremendous potential. Coming from a family steeped in boxing tradition he enjoyed the great support of his father, the ever present Jack, while brothers Les and Dennis also boxed professionally with Dennis beating Carl Gizzi to become Heavyweight Champion of Wales. Dennis went on to successfully defend his title against Del Phillips and Gene Innocent.

Eddie began his professional career as a middleweight with a six round points win over Dave Arnold on July 1st, 1963 at the National Sporting Club with stablemate Stuart Price also on the bill. In his second contest he beat the rugged Terry Phillips over six rounds at Coney Beach Arena, Porthcawl on the night when Howard Winstone defended his British title against Billy Calvert of Sheffield, and before the year was out he had won and lost against Joe Somerville, again at the National Sporting Club. During his first year in the paid ranks, four of his five contests took place at the Club, where he was to become extremely popular.

He went through 1964 undefeated in twelve contests beating the likes of tough Irishman Henry Turkington and Fitzroy Lindo, who had caused problems for Johnny Gamble from the same stable a year or so before. The momentum continued into 1965 but then Eddie was stricken with rheumatic fever which led to an enforced period of inactivity. When he returned to boxing in 1966 it was as a lightheavyweight and his winning run continued.

He began the year with a win over Lloyd Walford, a name which had already appeared on the record of Carl Gizzi and who would also appear later on the records of Roger Tighe and Roy John. He also notched up two wins over Charlie Wilson, a Londoner who frequently appeared at the gym in Penydarren as a sparring partner. Following another win over Walford, and after stopping Steve Richards and Clarence Prince, Eddie was matched with Derek Richards of Coventry for the Welsh Lightheavyweight title. The contest took place at Aberavon on July 12th and Eddie was beaten on points in a gruelling battle over ten rounds, and so his first title challenge ended in disappointment. Derek had won the Welsh ABA Middleweight title in 1962 and had represented Wales and was developing into a solid professional. He had lost to Chic Calderwood in a round but was stopped in the last round of a British title eliminator against Young McCormack. Just over a year later, McCormack defended his newly won title against Richards with the latter being knocked out in the seventh round, but Derek was the type of fighter who could make life difficult for any opponent and Eddie certainly had his hands full that night. Ironically, Derek was born in Merthyr, and over the years he caused more than a few problems for the Thomas stable.

Apart from his problems with rheumatic fever, Eddie was frequently troubled by cuts around his eyes. The problem became so acute that he decided to undergo an operation to attend to the bone structure and scar tissue around both eyes. Nowadays Eddie looks back at this in lighthearted fashion and blames Eddie Thomas for his appearance!

After the disappointment of his defeat by Derek Richards, Eddie returned with wins over Ernie Field and Johnny Ould. His last fight of 1966 came on December 7th at Aberavon when he beat the tough Togan Johnny Halafihi on points over eight rounds.

Eddie Avoth first challenged for the British Lightheavyweight title on Jun 19th, 1967. The title was vacant and this probably helped Les Roberts clinch the match for the National Sporting Club. Eddie was matched with Young McCormack and the referee stopped the contest in the seventh round after Avoth had been cut. He then marked time with wins over John Hendrickson, a tough opponent, and the awkward Nigerian Guinea Roger. This turned out to be a particularly bloody battle at Aberavon, and it was after this fight that Eddie underwent surgery on his eyebrows in an attempt to limit future damage. He returned to the ring in March, 1968 with a points win over John Hendrickson at the National Sporting Club and gave a repeat performance in April beating Hendrickson on points over eight rounds at Sophia Gardens, Cardiff. His next opponent was the American Stanford Bulla whom he beat on points over ten rounds on the night of July 24th, 1968 at Porthcawl when Howard Winstone lost his title to Jose Legra. His return contest with McCormack was scheduled for January 13th, 1969 when Eddie forced the Irishman to retire in eleven rounds at the World Sporting Club, thus capturing the British title and making history for manager Eddie Thomas by becoming his third champion. After wins over Lou Gutierrez and Lloyd Walford, he travelled to Zagreb in June to meet Yvan Prebeg for the vacant European Lightheavyweight title but was beaten on points over fifteen rounds.

He returned to action in October when he defeated Bunny Johnson on points over eight rounds at Nottingham. Johnson was not the most fashionable of fighters, but during the latter part of the seventies he won the British title at both lightheavyweight and heavyweight.

Early in 1970 there was call for a rubber match with Young John McCormack and this took place at Nottingham on April 6th. This time the contest ended prematurely with the Irishman being disqualified in the eighth round. Later in the year Eddie went over to America and lost on points over ten rounds to Mike Quarry. Mike was the brother of Jerry Quarry, who, at one time was being hailed as the new "Great white hope" and who will be remembered for his courageous battles against Muhammad Ali and many others.

Eddie's travels continued and in October he went to Brisbane to box for the vacant Empire title. On October 23rd, he defeated Trevor Thornberry in six rounds to claim the title, but there were some anxious moments for Eddie. The ending was dramatic and he floored Thornberry with a crushing right which left the Australian on the canvas for several minutes with Eddie extremely concerned for his opponent's well being.

Eddie Avoth needed only one more notch to win the Lonsdale Belt outright and on January 24th, 1971 he was matched with Olympic Champion Chris Finnegan at the World Sporting Club. Some months previously, Eddie had been involved in a serious car accident, after which he required over thirty stitches in the head wounds he had sustained and there was a feeling that he was returning to ring action too quickly. It turned out to be a torrid battle with the referee stopping the contest in the last round in Finnegan's favour and so the belt eluded Eddie, who was not at his best on the night. Chris became one of boxing's great characters and later defended his titles successfully against Roy John, who was also trained at Penydarren. He will always be remembered for his battles with John Conteh and his epic struggle against the legendary Bob Foster for the world title.

In May, Eddie was back in the ring at Caerphilly and beat old foe Guinea Roger over eight rounds, aiming to put himself back into title contention. This was manager Eddie Thomas' first promotion at the plush Club Double Diamond. He worked closely with businessman Bob Lewis and it was his ambition to set up an Anglo Welsh Sporting Club, run on the lines of the National Sporting Club in London. Eddie felt this would be the ideal venue where his plans could be brought to fruition and there were some successful nights, but fight fans in Wales have shown over the years that they preferred small hall boxing to the dinner show atmosphere.

After beating Guinea Roger, Eddie Avoth then went off to Johannesburg in June and outpointed Kosie Smith in a ten round contest but when he returned to South Africa in October he lost on points to Sarel Aucamp.

His last contest took place at Caerphilly when he was stopped in three rounds by Bunny Johnson at the Club Double Diamond on March 15th, 1972. Sensibly, he decided that now was the time to retire. He could look back on a successful career with his contests against McCormack standing out.

Eddie was probably at his best in the second contest against McCormack. The Irishman started the contest well and attacked Avoth's body and Eddie was in trouble on several occasions, but he came through the storm and from the fifth round on, he began to find his range with the left hand. He was now starting to throw powerful right hooks to McCormack's body as well.

By the end of the ninth round the contest must have been evenly balanced but Avoth then began to exert real pressure and in the tenth round he caught the champion with something like thirteen uppercuts. It is worth noting that at a time when the uppercut was not frequently used, boxers from the Thomas stable were actively encouraged to develop this punch.

The eleventh round was a fierce affair and after a barrage of punches from Avoth, McCormack was badly cut, though he still looked dangerous. Avoth was still prepared to trade punches but kept his cool and McCormack was obviously in distress as the round ended. His seconds examined the injury and then called over the referee, Roland Dakin, who stopped the contest, and so, after a gap of sixteen years, the Lightheavyweight Championship of Great Britain had returned to Wales.

There was always a great sense of fun when Eddie Avoth was training at the gym in Penydarren and there was always friendly banter between Winstone, Buchanan and Avoth. The arguments as to who was the prettiest seemed to go on for ever and there was an endless stream of practical jokes. Avoth was blessed with sublime skills and Eddie Thomas regarded him as one of the most gifted fighters he had trained but we can only speculate as to what he might have achieved had it not been for his illness and the susceptibility to cuts.

After retiring from boxing, Eddie turned his attention to various business ventures including the running of clubs, restaurants and bars. He lived in Spain for a time and ran the famous Silks in Marbella of which he was also a part owner. In recent years he has worked hard on behalf of the Welsh Ex-Boxers' Association, generously supporting the statue appeal funds for both Howard Winstone and Johnny Owen. In December 2002 he was granted Honorary Life Membership of the Association in acknowledgement of his support and he has also been honoured by the Variety Club of Great Britain. He is regularly invited to boxing functions all over the country. In his heyday he was always in demand for personal appearances and his popularity remains undiminished. He is always smiling, and always greets people with that incredible bear hug and the obligatory kiss. He is still the champ that everyone wants to talk to.

Eddie Avoth

Born: Cardiff, May 2nd, 1945
Welsh ABA Lightmiddleweight Title 1963
Welsh International
British Lightheavyweight Champion
Empire Lightheavyweight Champion

Professional Record

1963
Jul 1st	Dave Arnold	w.pts.6	London
Aug 20th	Terry Phillips	w.pts.6	Porthcawl
Oct 22nd	Ray Fallone	w.pts.6	London
Nov 25th	Joe Somerville	w.pts.6	London
Dec 9th	Joe Somerville	l.pts.6	London

1964
Feb 24th	Sid Brown	w.pts.6	London
Mar 24th	Henry Turkington	w.rsf.4	London
May 12th	Jack Powell	w.ko.6	London
May 20th	Dave Arnold	w.ko.4	London
Jun 22nd	Sid Brown	w.pts.8	London
Jul 20th	Louis Onwuna	w.pts.6	Ebbw Vale
Sep 21st	Jimmy Stewart	w.ko.1	Manchester
Oct 12th	Gary Chippendale	w.rsf.4	Manchester
Nov 2nd	Fitzroy Lindo	w.pts.8	Ebbw Vale
Nov 16th	Louis Onwuna	w.ko.2	Manchester
Dec 1st	George Palin	w.ko.1	London
Dec 14th	Tony French	w.pts.6	London

1965
Jan 20th	Roy Thomas	w.rsf.6	Cardiff
Feb 1st	Sid Brown	w.rsf.5	London
Mar 8th	Fitzroy Lindo	w.rsf.7	London
Apr 26th	Joe Bell	w.pts.8	London

1966
Jan 10th	Lloyd Walford	w.rsf.6	London
Feb 28th	Charlie Wilson	w.pts.8	London
Apr 4th	Charlie Wilson	w.rsf.1	London
Apr 19th	Lloyd Walford	w.rsf.7	London
May 11th	Steve Richards	w.rsf.4	Manchester
Jun 6th	Clarence Prince	w.rsf.2	London
Jul 12th	Derek Richards	l.pts.10	Aberavon
	(Welsh Lightheavyweight Title)		
Sep 19th	Ernie Field	w.pts.8	Manchester
Oct 26th	Johnny Ould	w.rsf.4	London
Dec 7th	Johnny Halafihi	w.pts.8	Aberavon

1967
Jan 30th	Ernie Field	l.rtd.2	Manchester
Jun 19th	Young McCormack	l.rsf.7	London
	(Vacant British Lightheavyweight Title)		
Sep 19th	John Hendrickson	w.rsf.3	Wembley
Nov 28th	Guinea Roger	w.pts.10	Aberavon

1968
Mar 8th	John Hendrickson	w.pts.8	London
Apr 24th	John Hendrickson	w.pts.8	Cardiff
Jul 24th	Stanford Bulla	w.pts.10	Porthcawl
Nov 18th	Curtis Bruce	w.rsf.6	London

1969
Jan 13th	Young McCormack	w.rtd.11	London
	(British Lightheavyweight Title)		
Feb 6th	Lou Gutierrez	w.ko.4	Liverpool
Mar 17th	Lloyd Walford	w.pts.8	London
Jun 28th	Yvan Prebeg	l.pts.15	Zagreb
	(Vacant European Lightheavyweight Title)		
Oct 27th	Bunny Johnson	w.pts.8	Nottingham

1970
Feb 16th	Emile Okee Griffith	w.pts.10	London
Apr 6th	Young McCormack	w.dis.8	Nottingham
	(British Lightheavyweight Title)		
Jun 6th	Mike Quarry	l.pts.10	Woodland H
Oct 23rd	Trevor Thornberry	w.rtd.6	Brisbane
	(Vacant British Empire Lightheavyweight Title)		

1971
Jan 24th	Chris Finnegan	l.rsf.15	London
	(British and Empire Lightheavyweight Titles)		
May 12th	Guinea Roger	w.pts.8	Caerphilly
Jun 12th	Kosie Smith	w.pts.10	Johannesburg
Oct 30th	Sarel Aucamp	l.pts.10	Johannesburg

1972
Mar 15th	Bunny Johnson	l.rcf.3	Caerphilly

Eddie Avoth: British & Empire Lightheavyweight Champion

4

Ken Buchanan

There can be no doubt that Ken Buchanan was one of Britain's finest boxers of all time and his achievement of winning a world title abroad speaks volumes. He brought back the title from furnace-like conditions in San Juan and went on to make an immense impression at America's Mecca of boxing, namely Madison Square Garden, so much so, that in 1970 he was awarded the Edward J. Neil trophy by the American Boxing Writers, beating off competition from Joe Frazier and Muhammad Ali.

Ken was born in Edinburgh on June 28th, 1945 and enjoyed a highly successful amateur career. He won the Scottish ABA Featherweight Title in 1964 and retained his title in 1965, when he also won the ABA title. He also represented Scotland many times and when he decided to turn professional there was a great deal of speculation as to who would be his manager. Many people felt that he might link up with fellow Scot Bobby Neill, the former British Featherweight Champion. Eventually, Ken chose Merthyr manager Eddie Thomas who at that time presided over a stable which included British and European Featherweight Champion Howard Winstone, lightheavyweight Eddie Avoth and heavyweight Carl Gizzi. This stable of boxers clearly showed the skills and values of champion maker Thomas and so Buchanan made his way to Merthyr.

I remember being at the gym in Penydarren and seeing Ken spar with Howard Winstone for the first time. Winstone was hugely talented and was preparing for a world title challenge and was in his prime but Ken made a lasting impression on me and I remember making a prediction to my father as we left the gym that night the Ken would win the world title at the first attempt, regardless of where the fight would take place.

The National Sporting Club was to play a significant part in the apprenticeship of Ken Buchanan and he clearly benefited from the matchmaking skills of resident matchmaker Les Roberts, a dour Yorkshireman whose knowledge of boxing and boxers was all embracing.

No one should underestimate the contribution of Les in Ken Buchanan's development as the Scot put together four stoppage wins starting with a two round defeat of Brian Tonks on September 20th, 1965 at the National Sporting Club. He followed this up with three more stoppage wins and ended the year with an eight rounds points win over Junior Cassidy, again at the Club.

The momentum continued into 1966 and I saw Ken box for the first time on July 6th when he beat Brian Smyth in the first round at Aberavon. I recall the feeling of huge disappointment because the contest was over so quickly and I had wanted a longer look at him.

He continued to accumulate wins over quality performers such as Ivan Whiter, Mick Laud, a regular visitor to Merthyr as a sparring partner to Howard Winstone, Phil Lundgren and the American Tommy Garrison, who was beaten on points over ten rounds at the Royal Albert Hall. By now, Ken had picked up his first professional title by beating John McMillan on points at Glasgow to win the vacant Scottish Lightweight title.

Ken's next appearance on a promotion in Wales came on July 26th, 1967 at the Afan Lido, Aberavon when he beat the Frenchman Rene Roque on points over ten rounds. On this occasion there was ample time to savour his boxing skills and it was clear that a British title challenge could not be far away. After stopping Al Rocca in the seventh round at the World Sporting Club, he was matched with Spike McCormack in a final eliminator for the British title at the National Sporting Club. The contest took place on October 30th, 1967 and Ken was the winner on points after twelve rounds so the path was now clear for a meeting with Maurice Cullen for the title.

Cullen had been British Lightweight Champion for two years and was a highly accomplished performer. At the time, there were many who felt that Ken was facing a tough task when they were matched on February 19th, 1968 at the Anglo American Sporting Club, but he showed maturity and composure in abundance. He stuck to his task and knocked out Cullen in the eleventh round to take the title in sensational style.

Ken felt he would now begin to command large purses but unfortunately this was not to happen just yet and in April he was back in action at the National Sporting Club where he beat the Frenchman Leonard Tavarez over eight rounds. He kept his career ticking over with three more low profile contests, but he was becoming disillusioned.

He began 1969 with a win on points over ten rounds against Frankie Narvez, again at the NSC, but by July, he could take no more, and after stopping Jerry Graci in a round at Nottingham he decided to retire from boxing and returned his Lonsdale Belt to the British Boxing Board of Control. For a time he returned to his original trade of joinery, free from the pressures of the fight game, but a turning point was to come in October 1969 when his mother died. Eddie Thomas arrived in Scotland for the funeral and following a discussion, Ken decided to honour the remaining period of their contract, but he also made it clear that he no longer wanted to train in Merthyr.

The unease which existed in the relationship between Ken and Eddie was now clear for all to see. Part of the reason for this arose out of Ken's frustration at having to box on sporting club shows for small purses, while secondly, he was not able to appear on major London promotions because Eddie was in disagreement with Mike Barrett, Mickey Duff and Harry Levene. There is no question that these three men were the major players in British boxing at the time and Eddie had to rely heavily on the services of people like Les Roberts to secure regular work for his boxers.

In January, 1970 an opportunity arose in Madrid where he met Miguel Velazquez for the vacant European title. Ken trained in Scotland for this contest and his preparations were far from ideal. On fight night Eddie invited Leicester manager Johnny Griffin to work in the corner and Johnny was honoured to accept. Griffin was in Madrid with his heavyweight Rocky Campbell, whose name appears on the records of stablemates Carl Gizzi and Roger Tighe.

The contest against Velazquez turned out to be close and Ken was adjudged to have lost on points at the end of fifteen rounds. This was not an unusual occurrence for a British boxer fighting in Europe at the time, but sadly, it marked the end of Ken's unbeaten record.

He kept busy with a repeat win over Leonard Tavarez, this time over ten rounds in London. He then beat Chris Fernandez in Nottingham, and on May 12th, he knocked out Brian Hudson in the fifth round at Wembley in defence of his British title. This was Ken's thiryseventh contest, and his first appearance at the venue since he won the ABA Championship there.

In September 1970 Ken was given the opportunity he had craved for some time. He went off to San Juan to challenge Ismael Laguna for the world title, but he and manager Thomas had to overcome a number of problems before they returned home with the title. There were worries over the local judges initially appointed to handle the contest and there were problems in the dressing room when Eddie was taping Ken's hands. Eddie had to respond in no uncertain terms when he was threatened by Cain Young, one of Laguna's team who lunged at him with a pair of scissors when Thomas ignored his comments regarding the positioning of the bandages. When they eventually entered the ring they were given the corner most affected by the blazing afternoon sun, but in the end, Buchanan overcame all the obstacles to win on points.

There were further problems when Ken returned home. He was now WBA Lightweight Champion but this body was not recognised by the British Boxing Board of Control, who were affiliated to the WBC, and all this added to Ken's sense of grievance.

On December 7th he was matched with Donato Paduano at Madison Square Garden. Ken was conceding a great deal of weight but won on points over ten rounds and delighted the Garden fans with his sublime boxing skills.

In February 1971 he was on his travels again. He went to Los Angeles and beat Ruben Navarro on points in a contest which was also recognised by the WBC. At last, Ken was beginning to earn well and was gaining the respect his talents deserved.

In September 1971 he was back at Madison Square Garden for his return with Laguna and he repeated his points win. It was in this contest that the legendary skills of Eddie Thomas played such an important part in enabling Ken to retain his title. His use of a razor blade to release blood gently from Buchanan's eye, which was swollen shut is today, almost beyond belief. The champion's other eye was also cut and without a cornerman of Thomas' stature, the title would have slipped away.

Ken's supreme fitness was a key element in this contest and during the last couple of rounds he turned from boxer to fighter to outfight Laguna and overcome his own injury problems, showing immense courage in the process. Referee Jimmy Devlin had been extremely concerned about Ken's facial injuries, and after the eleventh round, ringside doctor Edwin Campbell examined them closely. He spoke to the referee and it was clear they were contemplating a stoppage. Sensing the danger, Ken staged a magnificent rally and in the fourteenth round, he caught Laguna with a magnificent right to the body, the most hurtful blow of the entire contest.

At the final bell, the referee and judges had scored unanimously in Ken's favour, and by now it was becoming clear that he was a huge favourite at Madison Square Garden. The kind of ovation he received from the crowd there is rarely given outside the heavyweight division and his victory over Laguna earned him the accolade of "Fighter of the Month" from the Ring Magazine.

The undercard featured a fighter called Roberto Duran who was described in the Ring Magazine as "one fighter of special note, who will have to be watched as a possible future lightweight champion and a definite current threat." Prophetic words indeed, as Ken would eventually find out. In the chief supporting contest he overwhelmed local fighter Benny Huertas, knocking him out in just sixtysix seconds.

When their contract expired, Eddie and Ken sadly parted company. Thomas said that he had grown tired of Ken's attitude and felt he could take no more, thus bringing to an end a highly successful partnership, but it is also easy to understand Ken's frustration at having spent so much time earning small purses on the sporting club circuit and not having access to the major promotions, even though he was now earning record purses for the Lightweight division.

Ken's father Tommy had always been an influential figure in his son's development and he now took over the managerial reigns. When Ken returned to New York to defend his title against Roberto Duran, his chief second was Gil Clancy, the trainer long associated with Emile Griffith, the former World Welterweight and Middleweight

Champion. In October 2003 I had the honour of introducing Ken and Emile at a Civic Dinner in Merthyr and it was interesting to hear Ken speak of their sparring sessions and doing their roadwork together in New York's Central Park.

The young Duran was a fearsome warrior and stopped Ken in thirteen rounds at Madison Square Garden. His illegal tactics would surely have resulted in disqualification in a British ring, but referee Johnny LoBianco allowed the persistent infringements to go unpunished. Punches continued to be thrown after the bell sounded to end the thirteenth round and at this point Ken was again struck by a low blow. In a piece entitled "Boxing's Most Controversial Punches" by Dan Daniel, which appeared in the Ring Magazine, Daniel writes, "The blow to the groin was indicated, in ringside photographs, as most likely coming from the Panamanian's knee.

Buchanan hit the deck in apparent pain. Reporters saw the incident. But the one man who was supposed to be in the best position to spot it, LoBianco, said that he had not seen the misadventure". He then ruled that Ken was unable to continue and awarded the bout to Duran.

I have to say that as a referee, I find it unbelievable that Johnny LoBianco was unaware of Duran's dubious tactics. Even though his handling of the contest drew criticism, nothing should detract from the fact that Roberto Duran went on to establish himself as one of the finest lightweights of all time and it is true to say that he has become one of boxing's legends.

Ken then began to learn that without his title, he had no bargaining power and it soon became clear that Duran had no wish for a return contest. Ken then had to set about the long process of re-establishing himself. He went back to the Garden in September and forced ex-champion Carlos Ortiz to retire in six rounds. It seems strange that a British boxer had become such a favourite at Madison Square Garden, but Ken can look back on his record there with pride.

On January 29th, 1973 Ken beat Jim Watt on points at the St Andrew's Sporting Club in Glasgow to retain the British Lightweight title and in doing so gained outright possession of the Lonsdale Belt. Jim was something of a late developer and went on to become World Lightweight Champion, helped by Terry Lawless and Mickey Duff. After retiring from the ring Jim enjoyed success in business and he is now a regular member of the commentary team for Sky's boxing coverage analysing the technical aspects of boxing superbly.

In truth, Ken was now having to box anywhere and everywhere. After beating Hector Matta in London in March he then went off to Miami Beach, New York, Toronto and Copenhagen, but amazingly, he kept on winning and earned considerable respect for his performances.

In May, 1974 he went to Cagliari and knocked out Antonio Puddu in the sixth round to win the European title. In December he went to Paris to defend his title against old foe Leonard Tavarez and stopped him in the fourteenth round. Things were never made easy for Ken and during September he had been forced to relinquish his British title because the deadline for his officially ordered defence against Jim Watt clashed with his defence of the European title against Tavarez.

Ken's efforts were rewarded in February, 1975 when he travelled to Tokyo to challenge Guts Ishimatsu for the WBC title. It was always going to be difficult and Ken lost on points over fifteen rounds, once more in his opponent's backyard. And so, it was back to Cagliari for another defence of his European title, this time against Giancarlo Usai, with Ken stopping the Italian in the twelfth round.

Ken had now been boxing professionally for ten years and decided it was time to retire, but his deteriorating financial position resulted in a return to the ring in 1979, and by December of that year, he was in Copenhagen, challenging once more for his European title, this time against Irishman Charlie Nash. Ken was beaten on points and it was a signal that his career at championship level was effectively over. A few minor contests followed when he was beaten on points by men who could not have lived with him in the early years of his career. The sight of a champion in decline was more than former manager Thomas could take, and when Ken lost to Lance Williams at Wembley, Eddie found himself unable to watch the action.

When he finally retired, Ken's record of sixtyeight contests included sixtyone wins and seven losses. Of the losses, four were in championship contests, such was the calibre of the man. The other three defeats all came in 1981, his final year in the ring. His record is quite remarkable and his successful record abroad places him alongside the greats of the lightweight division. He was without question one of the finest boxers produced in Britain over the last fifty years and few have come close to equalling his achievements.

His left jab was immaculate and his movement about the ring, his ring generalship, was of the highest order. These attributes were combined with a mental toughness which made him difficult to beat. He showed an abundance of natural talent, the like of which cannot be taught. He was not the finished article when he came to Merthyr, but the environment there allowed his talents to blossom.

Life after boxing was not particularly kind to Ken but he is now back where he belongs. In June, 2000 he was inducted into the International Boxing Hall of Fame at Canastota, New York and when he returned there in 2001 he was belatedly presented with the WBA belt to commemorate his winning of the world championship. A second book entitled "Tartan Legend" has proved to be highly successful, and since the death of Howard Winstone, Ken has reaffirmed his connection with Merthyr. He worked extremely hard in support of the appeal fund for Howard's statue and made numerous personal appearances to help bring the project to fruition. He also supported the appeal fund for Johnny Owen's statue in the same way and returned for the stable re-union.

On December 12th, 2001 I refereed on a Paul Boyce promotion at the Manor Park Hotel, Clydach and Ken was the guest of honour. He appeared with his Lonsdale Belt, together with those awarded to him by the EBU, the WBC and the WBA. He enthralled the audience with a talk from the ring about his career and we were privileged to see a short extract of fight film. The crowd responded to him as only a Welsh crowd could and it was abundantly clear to Ken that he still has pride of place in Welsh hearts. He enjoys attending functions arranged by ex-boxers' associations and I have to say it gave me great pleasure to welcome him at the twentyfifth anniversary convention of the Welsh Ex-Boxers' Association in September 2001.

Ken has since been awarded Life Membership of the Association, along with Eddie Avoth and Lupe Pintor. As President of the association, I am delighted that the achievements of these great champions have been recognised, and especially so since Eddie and Ken were part of the remarkable success story emanating from the gym in Penydarren.

Ken has always enjoyed recognition in America, and it was only right and proper that he should be awarded the MBE by the Queen. He has been honoured by the Scottish Boxing Hall of Fame and finally, he seems to be gaining the recognition at home that he has always enjoyed in the States. It was something special for me in 2002 to witness the respect and adoration of the fans he enjoys in Canastota, where he deservedly takes his place alongside his fellow boxing greats.

In November, 2004, Ken returned to Merthyr for a Civic Dinner at which he received a scroll from the Mayor, Councillor David Phillips JP, proclaiming him to be an Honorary Citizen of the County Borough of Merthyr Tydfil. This honour was bestowed in recognition of his achievements in the ring, together with his efforts on behalf of the statue appeal funds for Howard Winstone and Johnny Owen and his other charitable work. It proved to be an extremely emotional experience for Ken and it was most appropriate that his old landlady, Mrs Myfanwy Jones, from Dowlais, was there to witness the event. Myfanwy had looked after Ken during the time he trained in Merthyr under the guidance of Eddie Thomas.

The evening culminated in an even bigger surprise for Ken. Some years ago Ken had lost the Ring Magazine belt awarded to him as undisputed World Lightweight Champion and this was the glaring omission in his belt collection. Phil Jones, the son of Myfanwy and lifelong friend of Ken, had met up with Jerry Haack, the director of Newport Marketing, Inc, the company which manufactures championship belts during his visit to Canastota in June 2004, and through their good offices it was possible to present Ken with a replica of his original Ring belt. The presentation was made by fellow Hall of Fame inductee, Carmen Basilio. It was my privilege to introduce the ceremony and both Carmen and Ken were in tears as the presentation was made. It was a special moment for both champions, but it was also special for those of us who were lucky enough to be involved.

And so, the belt collection of Ken Buchanan is now complete and I doubt that we shall ever see another British boxer able to match this. Ken followed the traditional path to a world title, but nowadays, with boxers able to challenge for minor belts, the British title, and also the European title are frequently overlooked. Thankfully, status mattered to the "Tartan Legend" and his place among boxing's elite is secure.

Ken Buchanan

Born: Edinburgh, June 28th, 1945
Scottish ABA Featherweight Champion 1964, 1965
ABA Featherweight Champion 1965
Scottish International
Scottish Lightweight Champion
British, European and World Lightweight Champion

Professional Record

1965

Date	Opponent	Result	Venue
Sep 20th	Brian Tonks	w.rsf.2	London
Oct 18th	Vic Woodhall	w.rsf.2	Manchester
Nov 1st	Billy Williams	w.rsf.2	London
Nov 22nd	Joe Okezie	w.rsf.3	London
Dec 13th	Junior Cassidy	w.pts.8	London

1966

Date	Opponent	Result	Venue
Jan 24th	Tommy Tiger	w.pts.8	London
Mar 7th	Manley Brown	w.rsf.4	London
Apr 4th	Tommy Tiger	w.pts.8	London
Apr 19th	Chris Elliott	w.pts.8	London
May 11th	Junior Cassidy	w.pts.8	Manchester
Jul 12th	Brian Smyth	w.rsf.1	Aberavon
Aug 6th	Ivan Whiter	w.pts.8	London
Sep 6th	Mick Laud	w.pts.8	London
Oct 17th	Antonio Paiva	w.pts.10	London
Nov 29th	Al Keen	w.pts.8	Leeds
Dec 19th	Phil Lundgren	w.pts.10	London

1967

Date	Opponent	Result	Venue
Jan 23rd	John McMillan	w.pts.10	Glasgow
	(Vacant Scottish Lightweight Title)		
Feb 14th	Tommy Garrison	w.pts.10	London
May 8th	Franco Brondi	w.rsf.3	Paisley
Jun 28th	Winston Laud	w.pts.8	London
Jul 26th	Rene Roque	w.pts.10	Aberavon
Sep 14th	Al Rocca	w.rsf.7	London
Oct 30th	Spike McCormack	w.pts.12	London
	(Final eliminator British Lightweight Title)		

1968

Date	Opponent	Result	Venue
Feb 19th	Maurice Cullen	w.ko.11	London
	(British Lightweight Title)		
Apr 22nd	Leonard Tavarez	w.pts.8	London
Jun 10th	Ivan Whiter	w.pts.8	London
Oct 23rd	Angel Garcia	w.pts.10	London
Dec 11th	Ameur Lamine	w.rsf.3	Hamilton

1969

Date	Opponent	Result	Venue
Jan 2nd	Frankie Narvaez	w.pts.10	London
Feb 17th	Mike Cruz	w.rsf.4	London
Mar 5th	Jose Luis Torcida	w.pts.8	Solihull
Jul 14th	Jerry Graci	w.rsf.1	Nottingham
Nov 11th	Vincenzo Pitardi	w.rsf.2	London

1970

Date	Opponent	Result	Venue
Jan 29th	Miguel Velazquez	l.pts.15	Madrid
	(Vacant European Lightweight Title)		
Feb 23rd	Leonard Tavarez	w.pts.10	London
Apr 6th	Chris Fernandez	w.pts.10	Nottingham

1970 cont

Date	Opponent	Result	Venue
May 12th	Brian Hudson	w.ko.5	Wembley
	(British Lightweight Title)		
Sep 26th	Ismael Laguna	w.pts.15	San Juan
	(WBA Lightweight Title)		
Dec 7th	Donato Paduano	w.pts.10	New York

1971

Date	Opponent	Result	Venue
Feb 12th	Ruben Navarro	w.pts.15	Los Angeles
	(WBC Lightweight Title)		
May 11th	Carlos Hernandez	w.rsf.8	Wembley
Sep 13th	Ismael Laguna	w.pts.15	New York
	(WBA Lightweight Title)		

1972

Date	Opponent	Result	Venue
Mar 28th	Al Ford	w.pts.10	Wembley
Apr 29th	Andries Steyn	w.rsf.3	Johannesburg
Jun 26th	Roberto Duran	l.rsf.13	New York
	(WBA Lightweight Title)		
Sep 20th	Carlos Ortiz	w.rtd.6	New York
Dec 4th	Chang Kil-Lee	w.rsf.2	New York

1973

Date	Opponent	Result	Venue
Jan 29th	Jim Watt	w.pts.15	Glasgow
	(British Lightweight Title)		
Mar 27th	Hector Matta	w.pts.10	London
May 29th	Frankie Otero	w.pts.10	Miami Beach
Sep 1st	Chu Chu Malave	w.rsf.7	New York
Oct 11th	Frankie Otero	w.rtd.5	Toronto
Dec 6th	Miguel Araujo	w.ko.1	Copenhagen

1974

Date	Opponent	Result	Venue
Feb 7th	Jose Peterson	w.pts.10	Copenhagen
Apr 4th	Joe Tetteh	w.ko.3	Copenhagen
May 1st	Antonio Puddu	w.ko.6	Cagliari
	(European Lightweight Title)		
Nov 21st	Winston Noel	w.rsf.2	Copenhagen
Dec 16th	Leonard Tavarez	w.rsf.14	Paris
	(European Lightweight Title)		

1975

Date	Opponent	Result	Venue
Feb 27th	Guts Ishimatsu	l.pts.15	Tokyo
	(WBC Lightweight Title)		
Jul 25th	Giancarlo Usai	w.rsf.12	Cagliari
	(European Lightweight Title)		

Announced retirement.

1979

Date	Opponent	Result	Venue
Jun 28th	Benny Benitez	w.pts.8	Randers
Sep 6th	Eloy De Souza	w.pts.8	Randers
Dec 6th	Charlie Nash	l.pts.12	Copenhagen
	(European Lightweight Title)		

1980			
May 15th	Najib Daho	w.ko.7	London
Oct 20th	Des Gwilliam	w.pts.8	Birmingham
1981			
Jan 26th	Steve Early	l.pts.12	Edgbaston
	(Final eliminator, British lightwelterweight title)		
Apr 4th	Langton Tinago	l.pts.10	Salisbury
Nov 24th	Lance Williams	l.pts.8	Wembley

Ken Buchanan: British, European & World Lightweight Champion

5

Gerald Jones

Gerald Jones was born in Merthyr Tydfil on November 5th, 1943. As a youngster he joined the Dowlais Amateur Boxing Club and represented them with distinction. He appeared regularly on the shows arranged by Eddie Thomas in nearby valley towns and villages. He became a Welsh international and won the Welsh ABA Flyweight Championship in 1961, the title vacated by Don James when he turned professional. Gerald provided Dowlais ABC with its second title of the night with John Gamble taking the Lightmiddleweight crown. A hat-trick for the club was foiled when Malcolm Price lost in the semi-final at Lightheavyweight, but their combined efforts secured the "Western Mail" Challenge Shield for the Dowlais Amateur Boxing Club.

Gerald's opponent in the final was Keith Davies of the Amman Valley and it has to be said that Gerald looked the stronger from the start, with Davies being floored by a cluster of body shots.

A left-right combination to the chin floored Davies for a second time and when he went down for the third time, the referee stopped the contest with only 2 mins 36 secs on the clock. Gerald had indeed captured the title in style!

It was a natural step for Gerald to join the professional ranks with his mentor Eddie and alongside his friends Howard Winstone, Johnny Gamble and Don James, and he made his professional debut on May 8th, 1962 at the Parc and Dare Hall in Treorchy. His opponent was the experienced Ron Elliott. Gerald, who weighed in at 8st 4lb, was much taller than Elliott and was by far the better boxer, but he was not afraid to mix it. It was during these periods of slugging that Elliott was most effective. It was a close contest and Gerald had to pull out all the stops to take the decision on points over six rounds in what Boxing News described as "a baptism of fire".

Barely a week later he was in action again at Oxford, but lost on points over six rounds to Mick Taheney but along with his stablemates, he was in action at Treorchy on June 22nd. His opponent was Frank Mennie, who crowded Gerald right from the start. It developed into a ding-dong battle with Gerald producing a storming finish to clinch the decision.

Eddie was very fond of Gerald and recognised his talent and all-round ability and he felt that with a little more luck he could have gone on to win a British title. He sparred countless rounds with Howard Winstone, in spite of the fact that Howard was much the bigger man and he was often asked by Eddie to test out some of the younger boxers who came along to the gym. One such fighter was Tony Williams, who enjoyed a very successful amateur career and who won the Welsh ABA Flyweight title in 1965. Tony's professional career was shortlived, but he went on to become Coaching Director for the Welsh Amateur Boxing Association.

Gerald's professional career stretched to thirty contests between 1962 and 1966, but there were four more contests during a short comeback in 1968. He lost to Billy Thomas in his fourth professional fight, retiring in the fourth round at Carmarthen and Billy would go on to become a frequent visitor to the gym as Howard Winstone's chief sparring partner.

Gerald featured on Eddie's bills at the Parc and Dare Hall, Treorchy, the Coliseum Theatre in Aberdare and the Indoor Cricket School at Ebbw Vale but he became a great favourite at the National Sporting Club. He was, in truth, a matchmaker's dream.

He was an all-action fighter whose courage was beyond question. He featured in some cracking contests against opponents such as Tommy Burgoyne and Sammy McIlvenna but he is perhaps best remembered for his three epic battles with Cardiff's Terry Gale for the Bantamweight Championship of Wales.

They met for the first time for the vacant title at the National Sporting Club on June 28th, 1965 with Gale winning on points over ten rounds. The return match in Cardiff in September 1965 ended in a draw and a third match between the pair was inevitable.

Their final meeting took place on July 12th, 1966 at Aberavon on the undercard of the contest between Carl Gizzi and Ray Patterson with Gerald finally capturing the title he so richly deserved when Terry Gale retired in the eighth round of what had become a gruelling battle. Gerald's performance was, as usual, characterised by grit and dogged determination.

After being stopped by Sammy Abbey at Torquay, it seemed that Gerald might retire. He was inactive during 1967 but came back in 1968 losing all four contests on points. By now, he was being looked after by former Cardiff heavyweight Roger Pleace who had always admired Gerald's fighting qualities. He advised Gerald that it was indeed now time to retire, though Gerald continued his involvement in the sport and became a highly successful and respected trainer at Dowlais ABC. Over the years he has produced several champions, and continues to do so working alongside John Gamble, Mark Virgen and Johnny Harris.

In September, 2002 the Welsh Ex-Boxers' Association presented Gerald with a belt in recognition of his championship win all those years ago and the pleasure of this modest man was plain for all to see. His award was thoroughly deserved as he has served the game so well for so many years.

Gerald Jones

Born: Merthyr Tydfil Nov 5th, 1943   Flyweight
Welsh ABA Flyweight Champion 1961
Welsh International
Bantamweight Champion of Wales 1966

Professional Record

1962
May 8th	Ron Elliott	w.pts.6	Treorchy
May 14th	Mick Taheney	l.pts.6	Oxford
Jun 22nd	Frank Mennie	w.pts.6	Treorchy
Jul 9th	Billy Thomas	l.rtd.4	Carmarthen
Aug 2nd	Ron Elliott	w.pts.6	Cardiff
Oct 29th	Graham Price	l.pts.6	Maesteg
Nov 12th	Graham Price	w.pts.6	Aberdare
Nov 22nd	Graham Price	w.pts.6	Swansea
Dec 27th	Graham Price	l.pts.6	London

1963
Mar 25th	Graham Price	w.pts.6	London
May 6th	Ron Elliott	w.pts.6	London
May 17th	Gerry Jones	w.pts.6	Bangor
Jun 7th	Gerry Jones	w.pts.6	Cardiff
Aug 6th	Ron Elliott	w.pts.6	Llanelli
Sep 20th	Tony Barlow	w.pts.6	Corwen
Nov 4th	Mick Taheney	w.pts.6	London
Dec 9th	Carl Taylor	l.pts.6	London

1964
Jan 28th	Carl Taylor	l.pts.6	London
Mar 16th	Gerry Jones	l.dis.3	Manchester
Apr 6th	Gerry Jones	w.ko.2	London
Jul 20th	Tommy Burgoyne	w.pts.8	Ebbw Vale
Sep 7th	Sammy McIlvenna	d.8	Ebbw Vale
Nov 2nd	Sammy McIlvenna	w.ko.3	Ebbw Vale
Nov 16th	Tommy Burgoyne	l.rsf.5	Manchester

1965
Apr 26th	Tommy Burgoyne	l.pts.8	London
Jun 28th	Terry Gale	l.pts.10	London
	(Vacant Welsh Bantamweight Title)		
Sep 23rd	Terry Gale	d.10	Cardiff
	(Welsh Bantamweight Title)		

1966
Apr 4th	Don Weller	l.pts.8	London
May 2nd	Ron Elliott	l.pts.8	London
Jul 12th	Terry Gale	w.rtd.8	Aberavon
	(Welsh Bantamweight Title)		
Aug 3rd	Sammy Abbey	l.rsf.5	Torquay

1967
Inactive.

1968
Apr 18th	Steve Elliston	l.pts.8	London
May 21st	Johnny Fitzgerald	l.pts.8	London
Sep 16th	Joey Wright	l.pts.6	Leamington
Oct 21st	Frank Fitzgerald	l.pts.8	Bristol

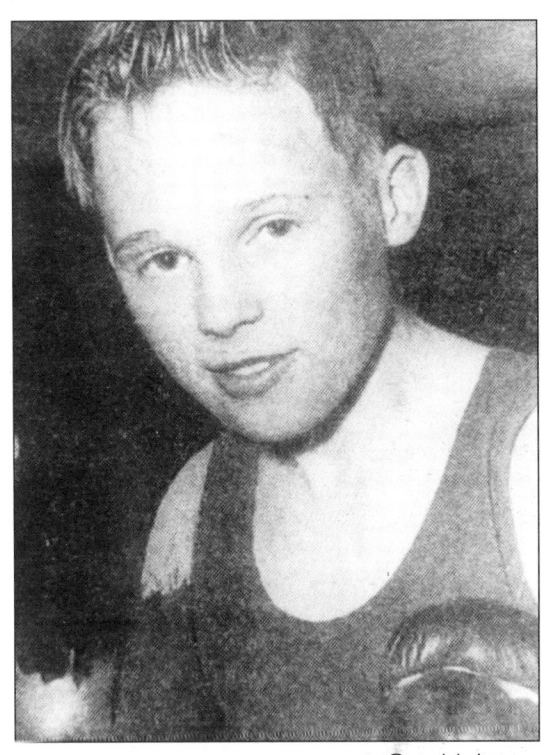

Gerald Jones: Welsh Bantamweight Champion

Stable-Members Re-Unite
(l-r): Ken Buchanan, Don James, John Gamble, Gerald Jones & Merthyr Businessman Bob Wilding

6

Carl Gizzi

Carl Gizzi was born in Rhyl on May 14th, 1944. As a young boy he suffered from polio but thankfully recovered and developed an interest in boxing. He represented Wales at international level and in 1964 won the Welsh ABA Heavyweight Championship. Whenever he boxed, his father Don, his mother and sister were always there to cheer him on and it was clear that they were extremely proud of him.

There was a great deal of excitement in Merthyr when he decided to turn professional with Eddie Thomas as the emergence of a big man sets people dreaming of "the richest prize in sport", the Heavyweight Championship of the World. Wales had also enjoyed success in this division with the names of Tommy Farr, Jack Petersen, Johnny Williams, Joe Erskine and Dick Richardson gracing the record books.

Carl began his professional career on June 30th, 1964 with a stoppage win over Billy Wynter and seven more wins followed before the year was out. His record features the names of all the journeyman heavyweights of the time including Cliff Purnell, a former opponent of Henry Cooper, Lloyd Walford, who seemed to be around for ever, and the tough Irishman Jim Monaghan.

Gizzi boxed eleven times in 1965 capturing the Welsh Heavyweight Title with a fifth round stoppage of Rocky James and he beat Dave Ould on points over eight rounds on the undercard of Howard Winstone's first challenge against Vicente Saldivar at London's Earls Court Arena.

He tasted defeat for the first time on April 19th, 1966 when he lost on points over eight rounds to Ray Patterson, the brother of former World Heavyweight Champion Floyd Patterson. Amazingly, this contest took place at the National Sporting Club on a tournament which featured two more boxers from the Eddie Thomas stable, namely Eddie Avoth and Ken Buchanan. Avoth beat Lloyd Walford on points and Ken beat Chris Elliott on points, both over eight rounds. It would be impossible these days to feature three talented stablemates such as Gizzi, Avoth and Buchanan on a low budget club show but Eddie Thomas and Les Roberts, the matchmaker at the National Sporting Club worked closely together over many years and clearly there was mutual benefit from this partnership.

Ray Patterson was based in Gothenburg and his style was similar to that of Floyd, working for his openings behind a long, stingingly accurate jab. Having inflicted Carl's first professional defeat, there was call for a return, but in June, Ray stopped Johnny Prescott, another of our leading heavyweights in five rounds at Wembley. Johnny was pinned on the ropes and taking heavy punishment when referee Bill Williams stepped between them.

The eagerly awaited return contest with Ray Patterson was staged on July 12th at Aberavon and saw one of Carl Gizzi's finest performances when he gained revenge with a win on points over ten rounds. Carl was at his very best in this contest. He was a skilful boxer and his left jab was solid. His movement around the ring was good for a big man, but if anything, he lacked what Eddie would have called a "wicked streak", that which others might call the killer instinct and the fact that he was a true gentle giant may just have prevented the breakthrough at the highest level.

In 1967 he beat the Italian Bepi Ros both in London and Treviso and beat Rocky Campbell in between. His fourth success of the year came on November 28th at Aberavon when he beat the American Hubert Hilton on points over ten rounds. Hilton was a good class fighter and had previously faced Henry Cooper.

On November 27th, 1968 Carl Gizzi was matched with Jack Bodell at Sophia Gardens, Cardiff in a final eliminator for the British Heavyweight Title. The contest was eagerly anticipated but ended abruptly for Gizzi. He suffered an eye injury early in the contest and the eye had swollen tightly shut when the contest was stopped in the second round.

In May 1969 he beat Bernard Thebault in Paris but then lost on points over ten rounds to the big American Jack O'Halloran, but his big chance was not very far away.

On October 13th, he was matched with Jack Bodell at Nottingham for the vacant British Heavyweight Title, Henry Cooper having relinquished the crown after the British Boxing Board of Control refused him permission to challenge Jimmy Ellis, one of Muhammad Ali's sparring partners, for the WBA Heavyweight title.

Jack Bodell was an awkward southpaw and it seems incredible that he should have outpointed the skilful Gizzi over fifteen rounds, but that was indeed the result and after this gruelling contest, the softly spoken giant seemed to lose his way career wise.

In 1970 he lost to Jimmy Richards in Johannesburg and was knocked out by Mario Baruzzi in Rome.

Carl had felt for some time that he was not getting enough exposure in Wales, and when his contract with Eddie Thomas expired in 1970, he joined the stable of Paddy Byrne. He ended the year with a comfortable points decision over Charley White at the Premier Ring Sporting Club and it was an important result because Carl was returning after a career threatening kidney condition.

In his first contest of 1971 he was beaten on points over ten rounds at the Royal Albert Hall by Joe Bugner. Carl had prepared for this contest at the famous Thomas a'Beckett gym in London's Old Kent Road. He had sparred with Bugner a few years earlier in Merthyr and felt good about his chances. They were both around 6ft 3in tall and Carl felt capable of out-jabbing Bugner. He also felt that the experience gained in his title fight against Bodell would be crucial. But in truth, this was a make or break contest for Carl and he went on to lose against Danny McAlinden and Richard Dunn, both future British Champions, and the signs were that his best days were behind him.

This was confirmed on October 11th, when he lost on points over ten rounds against Dennis Avoth, brother of Eddie, in London for the Welsh Heavyweight title and Carl subsequently retired.

Carl Gizzi may have been found wanting at the highest level but he enjoyed a good career and I, for one, will always remember the manner of his victories over Ray Patterson and Hubert Hilton.

Carl Gizzi

Born: Rhyl May 14th, 1944
Welsh ABA Heavyweight Champion 1964
Welsh International

Professional Record

1964

Jun 30th	Billy Wynter	w.rtd.3	London
Jul 20th	Cliff Purnell	w.rsf.2	Ebbw Vale
Sep 7th	Lloyd Walford	w.pts.6	Ebbw Vale
Sep 14th	Jim Monaghan	w.dis.4	London
Sep 21st	Jim Monaghan	w.pts.6	Manchester
Oct 26th	Joe Johnson	w.dis.6	London
Nov 2nd	Lloyd Walford	w.pts.6	Ebbw Vale
Nov 19th	Billy Wynter	w.pts.6	Cambridge

1965

Feb 1st	Jim Monaghan	w.pts.6	London
Feb 18th	Rocky James	w.pts.8	Dumfries
Mar 29th	Tony Smith	w.rsf.1	Carmarthen
Apr 8th	Jim Monaghan	w.rtd.7	Liverpool
May 17th	Al Roye	w.pts.8	London
Jun 1st	Ray Shiel	w.rsf.5	Wembley
Jun 28th	Rocky James	w.rsf.5	London
	(Vacant Welsh Heavyweight Title)		
Sep 7th	Dave Ould	w.pts.8	London
Sep 23rd	Jack Whittaker	w.rsf.3	Cardiff
Nov 25th	Roy Enifer	w.pts.8	Cardiff
Dec 14th	Mick Cowan	w.rsf.4	Liverpool

1966

Jan 24th	Ron Gray	w.rtd.5	London
Mar 22nd	Obe Hepburn	w.rtd.4	Blackpool
Apr 19th	Ray Patterson	l.pts.8	London
May 11th	Ron Redrup	w.pts.8	Manchester
Jul 12th	Ray Patterson	w.pts.10	Aberavon
Sep 8th	Renato Moraes	l.pts.8	London
Sep 26th	Jose Menno	l.pts.10	London

1967

Apr 17th	Bepi Ros	w.pts.10	London
Jul 11th	Rocky Campbell	w.pts.8	Liverpool
Oct 14th	Bepi Ros	w.pts.8	Treviso
Nov 28th	Hubert Hilton	w.pts.10	Aberavon

1968

Feb 19th	Lloyd Walford	w.pts.8	London
Apr 22nd	Billy Gray	w.pts.10	London
Nov 27th	Jack Bodell	l.rsf.2	Cardiff

1969

May 5th	Bernard Thebault	w.rsf.4	Paris
Jul 7th	Jack O'Halloran	l.pts.10	London
Oct 13th	Jack Bodell	l.pts.15	Nottingham
	(Vacant British Heavyweight Title)		

1970

Feb 28th	Jimmy Richards	l.pts.10	Johannesburg
Apr 10th	Mario Baruzzi	l.ko.4	Rome
Dec 2nd	Charlie White	w.pts.8	London

1971

Jan 19th	Joe Bugner	l.pts.10	London
Apr 28th	Danny McAlinden	l.pts.10	Solihull
Sep 22nd	Richard Dunn	l.pts.8	Solihull
Oct 11th	Dennis Avoth	l.pts.10	London
	(Welsh Heavyweight Title)		

CARL GIZZI

HEAVYWEIGHT CHAMPION OF WALES

Manager:
EDDIE THOMAS
Phone Merthyr 3127

54 TRELLEWELYN RD.,
RHYL
Phone Rhyl 51477

CHAMPIONSHIP
BOXING TOURNAMENT

Presented by CYRIL THOMAS

(Courtesy, Western Mail & Echo)

WELSH HEAVYWEIGHT CHAMPION, **CARL GIZZI**, WHO FIGHTS A RETURN BOUT AGAINST RAY PATTERSON

RAY PATTERSON (U.S.A.)

Tuesday, 12th July, 1966
The Afon Lido, Aberavon, Port Talbot

Official Programme — One Shilling

Promoter: Mr. Cyril Thomas
Matchmaker: Mr. Les Roberts

All Officials by B.B.B. of C.

NATIONAL SPORTING CLUB

BOXING TOURNAMENT
Tuesday, 19th April, 1966.
Boxing programme 8.30 pm

Programme

Bout 1
10 (3) Minute Rounds International Heavyweight Contest

Carl Gizzi v **Ray Patterson**
(Wales)   (U.S.A.)
Heavyweight Champion of Wales.   Brother of the Famous Floyd Patterson.

☐☐☐☐☐☐☐☐   ☐☐☐☐☐☐☐☐

Bout 2
8 (3) Minute Rounds Lightweight Contest at 12 stone 9 lbs.

Eddie Avoth v **Lloyd Walford**
(Cardiff)   (Chesterfield)
Winner of John Harding Trophy 1965. Lost only one bout in 29 Contests.

☐☐☐☐☐☐☐   ☐☐☐☐☐☐☐

Bout 3
8 (3) Minute Rounds Lightweight Contest at 9 st. 12 lbs.

Ken Buchanan v **Chris Elliott**
(Edinburgh)   (Leicester)
Former A.B.A. Champion undefeated in eight professional contests.   No. 1 Contender for Midlands Area Title

☐☐☐☐☐☐☐☐   ☐☐☐☐☐☐☐

Bout 4
6 (3) minute Rounds Welterweight Contest at 10 stone 8 lbs.

Brian Quinn   **Pat Walsh**
(Swindon)   (Hammersmith)

☐☐☐☐☐☐   ☐☐☐☐☐☐

Next Tournament Monday. 2nd May. 1966

and Preview of the Film
"THE NOBLE ART"
at 6.30 p.m.

7

Glyn Davies

Glyn Davies, from Llanelli, was born on March 11th, 1943. He became Welsh ABA Bantamweight Champion in 1962 and represented Wales at international level.

He began his professional career in 1963 with a third round stoppage of Bobby Mack in London and he became one of the great characters of the gym with his wicked sense of humour. He had nine contests during his first year in the professional ranks and again the name of Caerphilly's Billy Thomas appears on the record of a protégé of Eddie Thomas with Glyn and Billy sharing a win apiece, both over eight rounds.

As with Gerald Jones, Glyn Davies was to meet Tommy Burgoyne, beating him on points over eight rounds at Maesteg and Ebbw Vale in 1964 and there were several more common opponents such as Carl Taylor, Don Weller and Sammy Abbey.

Glyn was rapidly making an impression on the professional scene. On July 28th, 1964 he was matched with the former British and Empire Flyweight Champion, Jackie Brown, at Porthcawl's Coney Beach Arena on the undercard of Brian Curvis defending his British and Empire Welterweight titles against Bootle's Johnny Cooke. Jackie Brown beat Glyn on points over eight rounds and repeated his victory on November 22nd, 1965 in London.

The year 1966 began and ended with contests against Sammy Abbey. In January, Glyn stopped Abbey in the seventh round in London but on December 7th, Sammy turned the tables, stopping Glyn in the fifth round at Aberavon on the undercard of Howard Winstone defending his British and European Featherweight titles against Lennie "the Lion" Williams of Maesteg. Abbey gained the stoppage win this time with Glyn having sustained an horrific vertical gash through one of his eyebrows which required several stitches.

Glyn Davies kept himself busy with eight contests in 1967 and almost equally so in 1968 when he went off to Johannesburg and drew over ten rounds with Mike Buttle and later in the year he knocked out Jan Persson in five rounds in Stockholm.

A losing streak of nine contests began in 1969 and went on until 1971, but it is interesting to note the quality of the opponents during this time. He lost on points to Steve Curtis and Colin Miles for the Welsh Bantamweight title and on August 11th,

1969 he was stopped by Franco Zurlo in three rounds in Fiuggi. The Italian would soon go on to become European Bantamweight Champion.

He lost in five rounds to John McCluskey, the British Flyweight Champion, and was beaten in four rounds by Paddy Maguire who would go on to become British Bantamweight Champion.

It can be clearly seen that Glyn's defeats came at the hands of high calibre opponents and though his performances may have been somewhat inconsistent, he was always in superb physical condition, something which he has always retained. This has also been the hallmark of the fighters with whom Glyn has been involved as a trainer or manager in later years.

Glyn retired from boxing in 1971 but made a comeback in 1979, so his remarkable career spanned a couple of generations. What was even more surprising was that he finally won a Welsh title, still at Bantamweight when he stopped Pip Coleman in seven rounds at Ebbw Vale Leisure Centre on October 4th, 1979.

Shortly before this, incredibly, I had the pleasure of refereeing his contest against Paul Keers on May 10th, 1979 at Pontypool Leisure Centre. Amazingly, Glyn was now thirtysix years old and his opponent was exactly half his age at eighteen. The result was a draw over six rounds, but in the friendly banter which we have always enjoyed over the years, Glyn usually insists that he deserved the decision.

On March 19th, 1979 Glyn lost on points to Vernon Penprase, one of the new generation of Eddie Thomas' fighters with Glyn himself having ended his association with Eddie before he retired for the first time.

On January 22nd, 1980 Glyn was matched with fellow Welshman Johnny Owen at the National Sporting Club in London, the scene of many of Glyn's early contests. Johnny, almost inevitably forced Glyn to retire in the fifth round. Glyn was by now almost thirtyseven years old while Johnny Owen was at the peak of his powers as a fighter.

Glyn Davies continued to box and had another six contests before he finally retired in 1981 after being knocked out in the first round by Paul Huggins. His career spanned eighteen years during which time he had met the best fighters in Britain. He was a true craftsman in the ring and because of his supreme fitness, even at the latter end of his career, he could always be relied upon to extend up and coming young fighters.

Glyn had the knowledge, experience and personality required to become a good trainer and over the years he continued to contribute in this capacity, with his boxers all displaying the important and valuable hallmark of fitness while he himself derived great pleasure from running marathons and taking part in charity fun-runs.

Glyn Davies

Born: Llanelli Mar 11, 1943
Welsh International
Bantamweight

Professional Record

1963
Feb 4th	Bobby Mack	w.rsf.3	London
Mar 25th	Mick Marsh	w.dis.4	London
Apr 29th	Jackie Dillon	w.ko.1	Cardiff
May 17th	Mick Carney	l.pts.6	Bangor
Jun 7th	Billy Thomas	l.pts.8	Cardiff
Jun 24th	Frank Mennie	w.pts.6	Carmarthen
Aug 6th	Billy Thomas	w.pts.8	Llanelli
Nov 4th	Simon Tiger	w.rsf.3	London
Nov 25th	Carl Taylor	d.8	London

1964
Mar 19th	Tommy Burgoyne	w.pts.8	Maesteg
Apr 6th	Carl Taylor	d.8	London
Apr 27th	Don Weller	d.8	London
Jul 28th	Jackie Brown	l.pts.8	Porthcawl
Sep 7th	Tommy Burgoyne	w.pts.8	Ebbw Vale

1965
Oct 4th	Brian Bissmire	w.pts.8	London
Nov 22nd	Jackie Brown	l.pts.8	London

1966
Feb 14th	Sammy Abbey	w.rsf.7	London
Mar 21st	Carl Taylor	l.pts.8	Brighton
Jul 4th	Don Weller	w.pts.8	London
Sep 19th	Tony Barlow	w.pts.8	Manchester
Oct 12th	Ron Elliott	w.pts.8	Torquay
Oct 26th	W. van Cuylenburg	l.rsf.4	London
Dec 7th	Sammy Abbey	l.rsf.5	Aberavon

1967
Feb 21st	Sean McCafferty	l.rsf.4	Belfast
May 16th	W. van Cuylenburg	w.pts.8	London
May 22nd	Brian Bissmire	w.rsf.7	London
May 30th	Don Weller	w.pts.8	London
Jun 15th	Karim Young	l.rsf.2	Cardiff
Sep 27th	Patrick Mambwe	w.pts.8	Merthyr
Oct 16th	Patrick Mambwe	d.8	London
Dec 7th	Sammy Abbey	w.pts.8	Exeter

1968
Jan 22nd	Tony Barlow	w.rsf.3	Manchester
Mar 11th	Sammy Abbey	w.pts.8	Bedford
Apr 29th	Mike Buttle	d.10	Johannesburg
Jul 2nd	Kenny Cooper	l.pts.8	London
Sep 14th	Jan Persson	w.ko.5	Stockholm
Oct 23rd	Orizu Obilaso	w.pts.8	London

1969
Jul 2nd	Steve Curtis	l.pts.10	Cardiff
	(Vacant Welsh Bantamweight Title)		
Aug 11th	Franco Zurlo	l.rsf.3	Fiuggi
Sep 29th	Steve Curtis	l.pts.10	London
Oct 13th	John McCluskey	l.rtd.5	London

1970
Mar 5th	Bob Allotey	l.ko.2	Barcelona
Sep 22nd	Paddy Maguire	l.rtd.4	Belfast
Oct 19th	Colin Miles	l.pts.10	Aberavon
	(Welsh Bantamweight Title)		

1971
Jan 25th	John Mitchell	l.rsf.5	London
Feb 22nd	Billy Hardacre	l.pts.8	Aberavon

1979
Mar 5th	John Cooper	w.pts.8	London
Mar 19th	Vernon Penprase	l.pts.8	Haverfordwest
Apr 19th	John Cooper	w.pts.8	London
May 10th	Paul Keers	d.6	Pontypool
Jun 27th	Damien McDermott	l.rtd.3	Derry
Oct 4th	Pip Coleman	w.rsf.7	Ebbw Vale
	(Welsh Bantamweight Title)		
Oct 22nd	Dave Smith	l.pts.8	London

1980
Jan 22nd	Johnny Owen	l.rtd.5	London
Feb 28th	Steve Cleak	l.pts.8	Ebbw Vale
Jul 1st	Steve Cleak	l.rsf.5	Swindon
Oct 1st	Pip Coleman	l.pts.10	Swansea
	(Welsh Bantamweight Title)		
Nov 3rd	Dave Smith	l.rst.2	Hammersmith
Dec 8th	Paul Huggins	l.pts.8	Hastings

1981
Feb 16th	Paul Huggins	l.ko.1	London

PROGRAMME - SIXPENCE.
BILL LONG PROMOTIONS presents

BOXING

Indoor Cricket School, Ebbw Vale
Monday, September 7th, 1964

8 x 3 min. Rds. BANTAMWEIGHT CONTEST at 8 st. 8 lbs.

GERALD JONES
MERTHYR. This boy needs no introduction in this hall. Now No. 1 challenger for the Welsh Bantamweight Title.
— v —
SAMMY McILVENNA
SCOTLAND. This boy is confident that he can succeed where Burgoyne failed and beat Gerald Jones.

8 x 3 min. Rds. BANTAMWEIGHT CONTEST at 8 st. 8 lbs.

TOMMY BURGOYNE
SCOTLAND. Former Scottish Champion. Making a welcome return to Wales after his terrific contest in this hall with Merthyr's Gerald Jones.
— v —
GLYN DAVIES
MERTHYR. Rated No. 4 in current National Ratings. Challenging all Bantams.

HOWARD WINSTONE
MERTHYR. British and European Featherweight Champion, will box public work-out in preparation for his forthcoming contest with the Spanish Featherweight Champion in Manchester.

6 x 3 min. Rds. HEAVYWEIGHT CONTEST

CARL GIZZI
MERTHYR. Former Welsh Amateur Star. Unbeaten as a professional.
— v —
LLOYD WALFORD
SHEFFIELD. Strong K.O. puncher. Gizzi's hardest test to date.

6 x 3 min. Rds. HEAVYWEIGHT CONTEST

MALCOLM PRICE
MERTHYR. Local boy. Sparring partner to Chick Calderwood.
— v —
ROY SEWARDS
LINCOLN. Challenger to Midlands Area Title.

6 x 2 min. Rds. FEATHERWEIGHT CONTEST at 9 st. 2 lbs.

TERRY GALE
CARDIFF. Stable-mate to Welsh Featherweight Star, Billy Thomas.
— v —
J. KAZOWSKI
POLAND.

(A Seer Sports photo)

GLYN DAVIES (Llanelly)

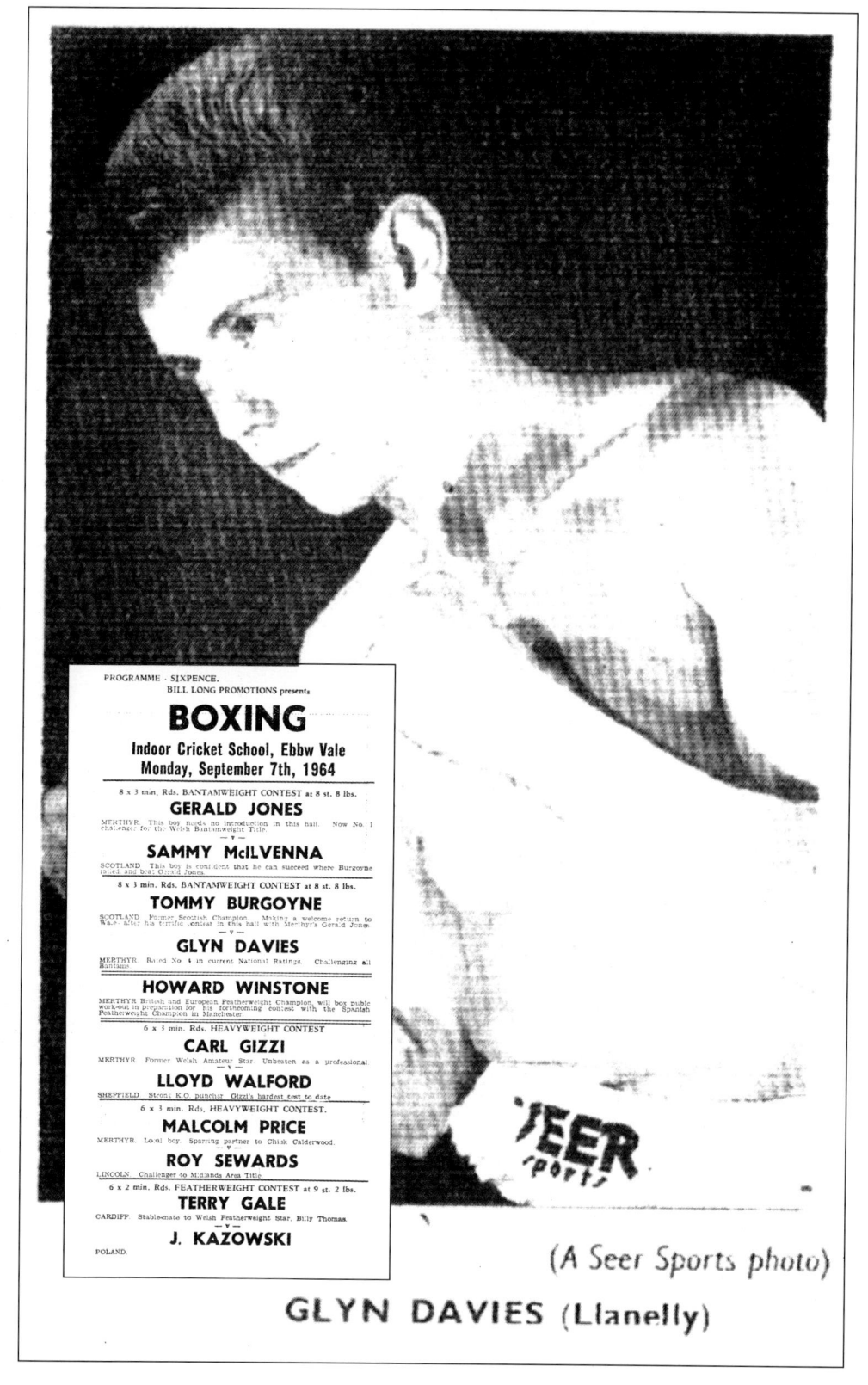

Glyn Davies: Welsh Bantamweight Champion

8

Roger Tighe

Roger Tighe was born in Hull on July 23rd, 1944. He enjoyed a hugely successful amateur career becoming ABA Lightheavyweight Champion in 1966, representing England at international level and winning the gold medal in the Lightheavyweight division at the Commonwealth Games in Kingston, Jamaica, also in 1966.

He turned professional later the same year with Eddie Thomas and was soon sparring at the gym with Carl Gizzi and Eddie Avoth. His first professional contest took place in Manchester on October, 24th and he beat Obe Hepburn on points over six rounds. Three more wins followed before the year was out. He beat Billy Wynter, a name which appears on the records of Malcolm Price and contemporary stable-mate Carl Gizzi. He then went on to beat Charlie Wilson on points. Charlie, who always seemed to be smiling, was to be a frequent visitor to the gym as a sparring partner and on December 14th, Roger forced Ron Gray to retire in three rounds in London. After he retired from boxing, Ron became one of the country's leading matchmakers and made a huge contribution to the sport over the years.

Roger tasted defeat for the first time as a professional when he was stopped by George Dulaire in the third round at Manchester on January 9th, 1967. He boxed another eight times during the year gaining revenge over George Dulaire, beating him on points over eight rounds at Aberavon on the night when stable-mate Ken Buchanan outboxed the Frenchman Rene Roque, and defeating Dulaire again on points in London later in the year.

On April 11th, Roger topped the bill at the National Sporting Club on the night when NSC members honoured Sir Alf Ramsey and the victorious England World Cup football team. Roger stopped Alex Kelly in the fourth round and the programme is an interesting piece of sporting memorabilia. It is a fold-open card shaped like a football with a picture of the Jules Rimmet trophy on the front.

On June 15th, Roger boxed on the undercard of the World Featherweight Championship contest between Vicente Saldivar and Howard Winstone at Ninian Park, Cardiff beating Rocky James on points over six rounds. Most of the preparation for this contest was done at Llanarth in West Wales where Eddie had set up a training camp and where former World Featherweight Champion Sandy Saddler was a visitor, though I suspect this was more of a publicity gimmick on Eddie's part rather than for any sound technical reasons.

The name of Lloyd Walford again appears on the record of a Thomas protégé and Roger was held to a draw by him at Leicester.

Roger opened 1968 with stoppage wins over Billy Wynter and Ron Redrup and in April he travelled to Gothenburg to meet Ray Patterson and lost on points after eight rounds. In 1969 Roger knocked out Bunny Johnson in six rounds in London. He stopped Lion Ven in the ninth round in Ghent and lost to Rocky Campbell on points over eight rounds in Hull in what was his first professional appearance in his home city, but he returned there in August to beat Bunny Johnson again, but this time on points over ten rounds.

During the year he boxed twice in South Africa, stopping Japie Pretorius in the fifth round and drawing over ten rounds with Jimmy Richards in Johannesburg on September 13th, in what was his last fight of the year. From this point onwards the career of Roger Tighe took something of a downturn and he would only record one more career victory. He boxed only once in 1970 and that was in Bilbao where he was stopped in the eighth round by Greg Peralta. The following year saw him make two ring appearances with a points loss and a draw, both against Rocky Campbell.

His only win came in 1972 against Dennis Avoth in London when Dennis was knocked out in the sixth round. Points defeats came at the hands of Richard Dunn and Bunny Johnson, both of whom later became British Heavyweight Champions and there was a points loss to Billy Aird who was a leading contender for the title. Billy Aird went on to become a manager after retiring from boxing and later became a successful referee.

Roger was inactive during 1973 and 1974 but he came back at the end of 1975 losing to Terry Armstrong and Peter Freeman, and when, on January 14th, 1976 he was knocked out by Freeman in the sixth round at Bradford in a contest for the vacant Central Area Heavyweight title his career was effectively over.

Following his glittering amateur career it seems that Roger Tighe did not fulfil his potential in the professional ranks. He was a boxer of no mean skill but probably needed a bigger punch to succeed at the highest level and maybe he was too laid back in his approach. In both the gym and the dressing room he always seemed relaxed and this may have prevented the breakthrough he desperately needed.

Roger is now a successful business man and was unfortunately not able to come to the stable reunion because of his commitments at the pub he now runs. It would have been fascinating to hear his views on the opponents both he and Carl Gizzi faced.

Roger Tighe

Born: Hull July 23, 1944
ABA Lightheavyweight Champion 1966
English International
Commonwealth Games Gold Medallist at Lightheavyweight, Kingston, Jamaica. 1966

Professional Record

1966
Oct 24th	Obe Hepburn	w.pts.6	Manchester
Oct 31st	Billy Wynter	w.pts.6	London
Nov 29th	Charlie Wilson	w.pts.6	Leeds
Dec 14th	Ron Gray	w.rtd.3	London

1967
Jan 9th	George Dulaire	l.rsf.3	Manchester
Feb 14th	Ian Hawkins	w.rsf.6	London
Feb 20th	Charlie Wilson	w.pts.8	London
Mar 7th	Obe Hepburn	w.pts.8	Manchester
Apr 11th	Alex Kelly	w.rsf.4	London
Jun 15th	Rocky James	w.pts.6	Cardiff
Jul 26th	George Dulaire	w.pts.8	Aberavon
Sep 18th	Lloyd Walford	d.8	Leicester
Nov 21st	George Dulaire	w.pts.8	London

1968
Jan 17th	Billy Wynter	w.rsf.6	Solihull
Feb 27th	Ron Redrup	w.rsf.3	Northampton
Apr 5th	Ray Patterson	l.pts.8	Gothenburg
Jun 25th	Vic Moore	w.rsf.5	London
Sep 23rd	Des Cox	w.pts.8	Bristol
Nov 27th	Rudolph Vaughan	w.rsf.5	Cardiff

1969
Jan 2nd	Bunny Johnson	w.ko.6	London
Jan 18th	Lion Ven	w.rsf.9	Ghent
Apr 3rd	Rocky Campbell	l.pts.8	Hull
Aug 8th	Japie Pretorius	w.rsf.5	Johannesburg
Aug 27th	Bunny Johnson	w.pts.10	Hull
Sep 13th	Jimmy Richards	d.10	Johannesburg

1970
Sep 1st	Greg Peralta	l.rsf.8	Bilbao

1971
Jan 13th	Rocky Campbell	l.pts.8	Solihull
Apr 26th	Rocky Campbell	d.8	Aberavon

1972
Jan 24th	Brian Jewitt	l.pts.8	London
Feb 14th	Dennis Avoth	w.ko.6	London
Mar 21st	Richard Dunn	l.pts.10	Bradford
May 9th	Billy Aird	l.pts.8	London
Jun 27th	Bunny Johnson	l.pts.8	Birmingham
Oct 18th	Lloyd Walford	l.pts.8	Bradford

1973/74
Inactive

1975
Nov 10th	Terry Armstromg	l.pts.8	Bradford
Dec 5th	Peter Freeman	l.pts.8	Blackpool

1976
Jan 14th	Peter Freeman	l.ko.6	Bradford
(Vacant Central Area Heavyweight Title)			

Roger Tigje pictured at the gym in Penydarren
Inset: The World Cup Winners Dinner programme
at the NSC featuring Roger Tighe & Alex Kelly

9

Gordon Davies

Gordon Davies was born in Brynmawr on January 11th, 1941. He enjoyed a successful amateur career, representing Wales at international level and winning the Welsh ABA Featherweight Championship in 1961.

He turned professional with Eddie Thomas and made his debut at the Miners' Hall, Merthyr Tydfil on December 19th, 1961 when he knocked out Arnold Bell in the fourth round. Gordon was a classy boxer with a solid punch and he went on to box eight times in 1962. He began the year by beating Peter Richards comfortably on points over six rounds in Cardiff but then on April 17th, he lost on points over six rounds to Johnny Mantle at Shoreditch. Johnny was a good class featherweight from Battersea who boxed many of the best British featherweights of the time.

Having experienced his first professional defeat, Gordon faced Peter Richards once more in his next contest on May 8th at the Parc and Dare Hall in Treorchy. Weighing in at 9st 2lbs Gordon repeated his previous victory, but floored Richards in the second, fourth and fifth rounds before having to settle for the decision on points.

On May 22nd, 1962 Gordon was matched with Lancaster's Frankie "The Tiger" Taylor at Wembley. The bill featured heavyweight Billy Walker, Terry Spinks, and the contest between Terry Downes and the American Don Fullmer, which Terry won on points over ten rounds. Frankie Taylor was already making his mark in the featherweight division and stopped Gordon in the fourth round. Gordon came to the professional ranks with a good amateur pedigree but I find it amazing that he was matched with Johnny Mantle and Frankie Taylor so early in his professional career. A young fighter thrives on the confidence which victory brings and Gordon was now having re-establish himself after these early setbacks.

Frankie featured in two high profile matches with Lennie "The Lion" Williams from Maesteg, beating him on both occasions, and much was made of the fact that here was a possible challenger for Howard Winstone. Frankie beat George Bowes in a final eliminator but never did get to challenge Howard because of an eye problem which forced him to retire from the game.

Gordon was another stable member who boxed on Eddie's promotions at the Parc and Dare Hall in Treorchy, the cinema in New Tredegar, the Coliseum Theatre in Aberdare and at Maesteg, winning on each occasion.

In May 1963 Gordon was knocked out in two rounds by Tommy Atkins at Bangor, but in his next fight on August 10th, he was matched with Teddy Best at Newtown for the Welsh Lightweight Championship. The result was a draw and so, unfortunately, the double of winning Welsh titles in both codes eluded him.

On August 20th, 1963 he was forced to retire in two rounds against Mickey Laud at Coney Beach Arena, Porthcawl on the night when Howard Winstone successfully defended his British and European titles against Billy Calvert of Sheffield, but he got back to winning ways stopping Tommy Blackwell in the first round at the National Sporting Club

Gordon recorded three wins and a draw from four starts in 1964 but in 1965, his only win out of four came against Brian Renney in Carmarthen on the undercard of Howard Winstone's contest against the American Don Johnson. After losing to Al Rocca on points over eight rounds and after being stopped in the sixth round by Tommy Blackwell, both at the National Sporting Club, Gordon decided to retire.

Following his retirement from boxing Gordon Davies became a successful trainer and it was a special pleasure for me to handle one of his protégés, Aneurin Williams, who made a good start in the professional ranks. I refereed two of Aneurin's contests and he later went on to win the Lightheavyweight Championship of Wales outpointing Chris Lawson, another boxer who started his professional career with Eddie Thomas.

I always enjoyed talking to Gordon in the gym back in the early sixties and we still enjoy a chat whenever we meet. He may have lacked the consistency required to succeed at a higher level but he still enjoyed a worthwhile career and was a valued and respected member of the stable, though I often wonder if his career would have taken a different path had he not been matched with Mantle and Taylor in those first few months in the professional ranks.

Gordon Davies

Born: Brynmawr Jun 11th, 1941
Welsh ABA Featherweight Champion 1961
Welsh International

Professional Record

1961

Dec 19th	Arnold Bell	w.ko.4	Merthyr

1962

Jan 29th	Peter Richards	w.pts.6	Cardiff
Apr 17th	Johnny Mantle	l.pts.6	London
May 8th	Peter Richards	w.pts.6	Treorchy
May 22nd	Frankie Taylor	l.rsf.4	Wembley
Sep 24th	Johnny Brown	w.rtd.6	New Tredegar
Oct 29th	Pat Aaron	w.pts.6	Maesteg
Nov 12th	Tommy Tiger	w.pts.8	Aberdare
Nov 19th	Joe Falcon	l.pts.8	London

1963

May 17th	Tommy Atkins	l.ko.2	Bangor
Aug 10th	Teddy Best (Welsh Lightweight Title)	d.10	Newtown
Aug 20th	Mick Laud	l.rtd.2	Porthcawl
Dec 9th	Tommy Blackwell	w.rsf.1	London

1964

Mar 16th	Al Rocca	w.pts.8	Manchester
Jul 20th	Tommy Tiger	w.pts.8	Ebbw Vale
Sep 29th	Billy Secular	d.8	London
Oct 12th	Freddie King	w.rtd.7	London

1965

Feb 15th	Billy Secular	l.rtd.4	Bristol
Mar 29th	Brian Rennie	w.rsf.4	Carmarthen
May 17th	Al Rocca	l.pts.8	London
May 31st	Tommy Blackwell	l.rsf.6	London

10

Malcom Price

Malcolm Price was born in Merthyr Tydfil on February 1st, 1943. He started boxing somewhat reluctantly but eventually enjoyed an extremely successful amateur career. He became Welsh Schoolboy Champion, then Welsh Youth Champion and later went on to win the Welsh NCB and ATC Championships and won the British version of the latter. He also represented Wales at international level.

I can remember seeing him box against Holland at the Hoover Factory canteen at Pentrebach, Merthyr Tydfil. The date was October 26th, 1961 and he outpointed A. Jongeneel. Also in the team that night was Stuart Price, who would soon become a fellow stable member, and boxing at lightmiddleweight was Derek Richards of Coventry who would prove to be a difficult opponent for both Stuart and Eddie Avoth in the professional ranks.

I saw Malcolm box several times as an amateur representing the Dowlais ABC, not only at the Hoover factory but at the Teddington Aircraft Controls factory in Cefn Coed and the Miners' Hall in Merthyr. As an amateur, Malcolm got on particularly well with Hughie Thomas, brother of Eddie, and I can remember sitting in the changing room with them shortly before a contest. The atmosphere was so calm with Malcolm sitting there placidly, but obviously focussed on the job in hand, while Hughie went about his preparations for the contest speaking quietly to Malcolm. He was obviously the master at motivating the boxer in his unique way and was a great builder of confidence, but quite different from Eddie.

Hughie had been a very good amateur boxer winning the NCB Bantamweight title in 1948 and winning the Welsh ABA title the same year. As a professional, his career seemed quite promising, but was cut short by persistent stomach problems, though potentially, my grandfather always insisted that Hughie could have been better than Eddie. He won the Welsh Bantamweight title at the Market Hall, Abergavenny on May 26th, 1952 forcing Roy Ball to retire in eight rounds but he later relinquished the title. On October 26th, 1953 he challenged Haydn Jones for the Welsh Featherweight title in Cardiff and was outpointed over twelve rounds.

In later years, when Malcolm's troubles made the newspapers I found it difficult to understand how this could be the same person, for on fight night he had always seemed so calm and disciplined. In truth, a lovely guy.

In his recent book "Street Warrior", written in conjunction with Steve Richards, Malcolm talks at length of his difficult relationship with his father. The boxing ring is one of the toughest of sporting arenas, but the fear of a parental beating following defeat in the ring is almost beyond belief. Such was Malcolm's fear of his father that he did not want to be dropped off at his house after losing a contest. I had heard this previously and the story is confirmed in his book.

I was at the Coliseum Theatre in Aberdare when he made his professional debut against Prince Croull on November 12th, 1962 when he won by knockout in the fifth round. This was an encouraging start, but his boxing licence was soon suspended following problems outside the ring and he did not box again until May, 1964.

He boxed five times during the year stopping Billy Wynter, Roy Sewards and Cliff Purnell and losing twice on points to the big Irishman Jim Monaghan, but at least he had the honour of facing Monaghan on the second occasion at London's National Sporting Club, the home of boxing.

I saw his contests against Roy Sewards and Cliff Purnell at the Indoor Cricket School at Ebbw Vale. They were both good stoppage victories. Sewards was an experienced professional who had been in with some good fighters while Purnell was a former opponent of Henry Cooper.

By now, I too was becoming an experienced programme seller, but I have special reason to remember the shows at the Indoor Cricket School because it was on one of these nights that I first sat next to "Star" referee Ike Powell, who was not on duty, but at the end of each round he would take out a postcard from his pocket and write down his own scores. Ike, from Bargoed, had been the leading Welsh referee for many years and had been upgraded to "Star" class following his handling of the contest between Randolph Turpin and Jean Stock at Leicester on March 19th, 1951. During the 1960's, he wrote a weekly column for the Daily Express and the card he took from his pocket had Ike's "Express" logo on it. It was the mystique of the scoring process which triggered my imagination and set me off a few years later on my quest for a referee's licence.

Unfortunately for Malcolm, more trouble outside the ring brought about the permanent withdrawal of his boxing licence. His reputation as a hard man was rapidly gaining momentum and brought about the inevitable consequence of periods in prison, but sadly, we can only ponder on what might have been in any assessment of his career.

Malcolm had cut himself off from the boxing scene over the years but I was delighted to be able to introduce him at the stable re-union. He refers to this introduction in his recent book and the sense of pride he felt in taking his place alongside his former stablemates. They were all greeted by thunderous applause and reading of the effect this had on Malcolm gave me too, a special pleasure. The people of Merthyr have always had a special place in their hearts for true fighters. .

Malcolm Price

Born: Merthyr Tydfil Feb 1st, 1943
Welsh Schoolboy Champion
Welsh Youth Champion
Welsh NCB and ATC Champion
British ATC Champion
Welsh International

Professional Record

1962

Nov 12th	Prince Croull	w.ko.5	Aberdare

1964

May 19th	Billy Wynter	w.rsf.5	Penarth
Sep 7th	Roy Sewards	w.rsf.5	Ebbw Vale
Oct 12th	Jim Monaghan	l.pts.6	Manchester
Oct 27th	Jim Monaghan	l.pts.6	London
Nov 2nd	Cliff Purnell	w.rsf.4	Ebbw Vale

Malcolm Price pictured far left of front row
(courtesy of The Western Mail)

11

Dai Gardiner

Dai Gardiner was born on March 1st, 1941 and as a youngster showed a great deal of interest in boxing. He represented Wales and in 1962 he won the Welsh ABA Lightweight Championship.

As an amateur he was looked after by Ray Gabriel who was himself Welsh ABA Flyweight Champion in 1956. Ray became one of the great characters of the Welsh Ex-Boxers' Association and was a familiar figure with his walking stick. He took great delight in visiting other Ex-Boxers' Associations the length and breadth of the country and Dai has always retained a special affection for him.

When he turned professional in 1962, Dai Gardiner joined the stable of Eddie Thomas. He lost his first contest at Newtown when he was stopped in the second round by Jimmy Mitchell but he beat Ron Rowley in his next contest at New Tredegar and then boxed four times in 1963 with one of these appearances at the National Sporting Club.

On June 7th he boxed Terry Phillips in Cardiff. Phillips was a tough, rugged fighter and Dai had to give away a great deal of weight, with the result that he was held to a draw over six rounds. This, unfortunately, was to be his final contest.

I saw a couple of Dai's contests and enjoyed seeing him train at the gym, where he always seemed to approach his work in a quiet, dignified manner. Just when his career was beginning to gain momentum he suffered a freak accident in the gym. He fell out of the ring and damaged his back. Some time later it emerged that he was suffering from a retina problem and he was forced to retire, a shattering blow for one so young.

He soon developed an interest in training and enjoyed remarkable success with boxers such as Wayne Bennett, Billy Vivian and Jeff Pritchard each winning Welsh ABA titles. He then turned to managing a professional stable and worked with several boxers before his first real success came with Johnny Owen. Dai worked closely with local promoter Heddwyn Taylor in providing opportunities for Johnny to box locally and there were some great nights, notably at Ebbw Vale Leisure Centre where I once had the pleasure of refereeing one of Johnny's contests.

With Dai's background in the sport it was hardly surprising that his boxers were so well conditioned when they came to the ring. Dai had sparred many rounds with Howard Winstone and often did his roadwork with him. He came to appreciate the importance of changing sparring partners after a couple of rounds and then bringing a boxer back later. He absorbed so much from Eddie and Howard, but with time and experience he was able to add his own dimensions to this fascinating process of preparing boxers for the demands of the ring and he was always pleased that his stable was usually large enough to ensure quality sparring for all.

Johnny Owen won the British Bantamweight title when he stopped Paddy Maguire in the eleventh round at the National Sporting Club, thus maintaining the Merthyr connection with the home of boxing. Dai later steered Johnny to the Commonwealth and European titles, but tragedy was to strike when Johnny challenged Lupe Pintor for the world title in Los Angeles.

Dai had looked after Johnny in much the same way that Eddie Thomas looked after his fighters, but Johnny's death came as a shattering blow to him and he drifted from the scene for a few years. As time passed, he gradually found his way back into boxing and enjoyed remarkable success with Robbie Regan and Steve Robinson. He steered Robbie to the British and European Flyweight titles and after challenging unsuccessfully for the WBO Flyweight title he moved up to bantamweight and took the WBO title from Daniel Jimenez on an emotional night in Cardiff in April, 1996. But again, tragedy was to strike. Robbie failed the required brain scan and had to retire from boxing on the eve of his first title defence.

Perhaps Dai's most remarkable success came with Steve Robinson who was given an opportunity at short notice to box for the WBO Featherweight title. He faced John Davison for the title after only fortyeight hours notice, when the champion, Ruben Palacio had to withdraw after failing the compulsory HIV test.

Dai's experience proved invaluable and Steve, who had lived in the shadow of Robbie for so long, went on to defend his title successfully seven times, beating former champions Colin McMillan, Duke McKenzie and Paul Hodkinson along the way. Steve then faced the bitter disappointment of losing his title to Naseem Hamed in Cardiff on an occasion made worse by the fact that Hamed's antics had really alienated Welsh fight fans.

To his eternal credit, Steve got over the humiliation of the Hamed experience and came back to win the European Featherweight Championship. After retiring from boxing he moved into training and with Dai's assistance has taken Dazzo Williams to the British Featherweight title. And so, as a manager, Dai emulated the achievements of Eddie Thomas, and like Eddie, he too has kept the game alive in Wales by promoting shows himself, and also in partnership with Robert Morris of Empress Cars. It was a huge loss to Welsh boxing when Robert sold his business and moved to Spain.

Over the years Dai has scaled the heights in boxing but he has also experienced the despair and the tragedy which the game throws up from time to time. I have always enjoyed a good relationship with him and I have refereed his boxers on many occasions. Decisions do not always please those closest to the action but Dai understands my position as a referee and we get on well together.

Little did I realise as a youngster watching him train that one day I would be officiating in so many contests featuring his boxers. As with Eddie, Dai has always been very good in dealing with cuts and I have to say that as a cornerman, he shows the kind of compassion that many do not have. He knows from experience that there are far worse things in life than pulling a boxer out of a contest.

When the Welsh Area Council of the British Boxing Board of Control celebrated its fiftieth anniversary in 1979, Eddie was honoured as the person who had contributed most to boxing during that period. Since that time, the achievements of Dai Gardiner clearly rank alongside those of his old mentor, and perhaps of even more significance is the fact that the influence of the Class of the 60s has extended into the twentyfirst century.

Dai Gardiner (Left) pictured with Steve Robinson, Dazzo Williams & Referee Wynford Jones

Dai Gardiner

Born: Cefn Fforest, Mar 1st, 1941
Welsh ABA Lightweight Champion 1962
Welsh International

Professional Record

1962
Aug 18th	Jimmy Mitchell	l.rsf.2	Newtown
Sep 24th	Ron Rowley	w.pts.6	New Tredegar

1963
Mar 26th	Harry Wheeler	l.pts.4	Wembley
Apr 29th	Jack O'Brien	w.rsf.4	Cardiff
May 6th	Peter Morgan	w.pts.6	London
May 17th	Howell Roberts	w.pts.6	Bangor
Jun 7th	Terry Phillips	d.6	Cardiff

DAI GARDNER (Cefn Hengoed)
Welterweight

Manager: Eddie Thomas
Gladys St., Pant, Dowlais,
Merthyr

Copyright Photo: Tommy Rees
68 Castle St., Caerphilly,
Glam

12

Dai Harris

Dai Harris was born in Merthyr on January 2nd, 1942. He won a Welsh ABA Junior title, a Welsh Army Cadet title and was National Coal Board Champion at Lightweight in 1960.

Dai established himself as one of the characters in Eddie's stable. In the gym he was usually at his funniest during sparring sessions and always seemed to be complaining to Eddie about the tactics of his sparmates and wanting to avoid Howard at all costs, while Don James recalls that he would never skip, one of the longstanding rituals of a fighter's preparation. Outside the ring he seemed to work quite hard at cultivating the perfect teddy-boy look.

He made his professional debut on December 19th, 1961 at the Miners' Hall in Merthyr beating Ron Rowley on points. I used to enjoy watching Dai in the gym and in contests but I can remember even in this contest, his antics annoyed the referee, Joe Morgan. I was relieved when Dai got the decision because Joe did not tolerate any nonsense in the ring. I got to know Joe well during the latter years of his refereeing career and we worked several shows together. I always enjoyed those occasions because I often felt we looked for the same things in a fight. He was an excellent referee and was desperately unlucky not to be upgraded to Star Class.

During 1962, Dai was extremely busy, the busiest boxer in the stable in fact, notching up thirteen contests with many of them on the undercards of some high-profile promotions. The first of these was on January 9th, when he appeared at the Royal Albert Hall. The bill featured stablemates Howard Winston and Johnny Gamble. Howard beat Oripes Dos Santos on points over eight rounds while Gamble stopped Johnny West in the second round, but unfortunately for Dai, he was forced to retire in three rounds against Tommy Blackwell, of Brixton. Dai began the contest well enough, but he sustained cuts above and below the left eye and he was pulled out at the end of the third round.

He was in action again on January 29th when he was matched with Peter Delbridge at the Drill Hall in Dumfries Place, Cardiff. Dai rushed in from the opening bell and took Delbridge completely out of his stride, flooring him several times. After two more counts in the fifth round, the referee stopped the fight. His performance was both colourful and courageous and there is no doubt that the fans found him exciting to watch. They always warmed to his all-action style.

His rematch with Don McCrae was typical of Dai`s crowd-pleasing efforts. Having taken every round up to the fifth, the referee stopped the contest with McCrae taking two counts during the round.

Over the next few months Dai appeared on almost all the shows that Eddie staged at local cinemas and theatres in South Wales and he started to put together a solid unbeaten run, though some of the contests were quite demanding.

On May 30th, he beat George Hand on points over six rounds at Cardiff's Maindy Stadium. Top of the bill was Howard Winstone defending his British Featherweight title against local man Harry Carroll. Harry was forced to retire in six rounds and Howard gained outright possession of his first Lonsdale Belt. This was a special night for me because it was the first time for me to see a British title fight. There was a large crowd at Maindy Stadium, a venue that was often used for athletics and cycle racing. It was also my first open-air show and I shall never forget the excitement of those few minutes before the title fight when the boxers made their way to the ring, picked out of the darkness by a powerful searchlight, and the thrill of all this going on to the sound of the Jack Solomons fanfare. I was already hooked on big-time boxing, and seeing Howard and Eddie approach the ring in a pool of light was a sight that I shall always remember.

On June 22nd, he beat Bob Sempey on points over six rounds at Treorchy. Sempey, from Belfast, found Dai difficult to handle at first and found himself on the receiving end of some impressive left jabs, but he was soon able to remind Dai of his own power and a big right caused a cut inside Dai`s mouth. The contest was a real thriller from start to finish and Dai emerged with the decision.

Following his win over Sempey and then beating Johnny Brown at Carmarthen, Dai was back in action on another Winstone undercard at Sophia Gardens, Cardiff on August 2nd. He beat Joey Burns on points over six rounds while Howard totally mesmerised Dennis Adjei. Johnny Gamble was also on the bill but lost to Fitzroy Lindo.

On September 11th, Dai drew with Mickey Laud at Wembley. This was a bill which featured Brian Curvis against the American Ralph Dupas with Brian winning on a disqualification in the sixth round, while Howard was also in action, stopping the highly touted Billy "The Kid" Davis in the seventh round.

Dai`s last fight of the year came on October 1st at Cardiff when he lost on points over eight rounds to Al Keen. Keen was a good fighter and this turned into a gruelling battle for Dai. He began to reflect on some of the matches he was having to take and became disillusioned with the sport thus prompting his decision to retire from boxing.

For many, boxing in the Lightweight division at this time in Britain would have been a daunting experience. Dave Charnley became British Champion in 1957 and dominated the division for seven years. I always felt he was special, but I also feel he was underrated. Dave was desperately unlucky in coming up against an exceptional world champion in the form of Joe "Old Bones" Brown, though he did beat Brown after Joe had been relieved of his world title. Dave had completely overwhelmed David "Darkie" Hughes from Cardiff in a single round at Nottingham and fighters of the calibre of Sammy McSpadden and Maurice Cullen were striving to break through, so it is easy to understand how someone might become disheartened.

Dai came from a large family and times were undoubtedly hard for him as a youngster. Though he may have lacked the absolute dedication required to succeed at the highest level in boxing he was always hard working, and much of this was physically demanding, which perhaps partly explains his early death at the age of 49, sadly, from a heart attack.

In his comparatively short career Dai was a busy fighter and had tasted the big occasion. He was the type of fighter which matchmakers depend on to maintain interest and to keep the game alive. Boxing has always needed great characters like Dai Harris, but sadly, today, there are not many of them around.

Dai Harris

Born: Merthyr Tydfil Jan 2, 1942
Welsh ABA Junior Title
NCBABA Champion at Lightweight 1959/60

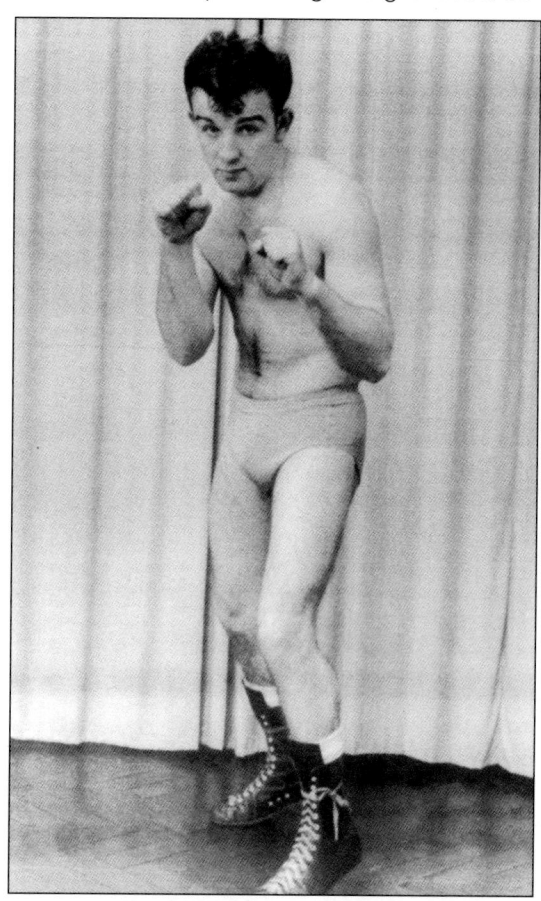

Professional Record

1961

Date	Opponent	Result	Venue
Dec 19th	Ron Rowley	w.pts.4	Merthyr

1962

Date	Opponent	Result	Venue
Jan 9th	Tommy Blackwell	l.rtd.3	London
Jan 29th	Peter Delbridge	w.rsf.5	Cardiff
Feb 12th	Ron Rowley	w.pts.6	Maesteg
Feb 26th	Don McCrae	w.ko.4	Merthyr
May 8th	Don McCrae	w.rsf.5	Treorchy
May 14th	Brian Brown	w.rsf.2	Oxford
May 30th	George Hand	w.pts.6	Cardiff
Jun 22nd	Bob Sempey	w.pts.6	Treorchy
Jul 9th	Johnny Brown	w.pts.6	Carmarthen
Aug 2nd	Joey Burns	w.pts.6	Cardiff
Sep 11th	Mick Laud	d.6	Wembley
Sep 24th	Bob Sempey	w.pts.8	New Tredegar
Oct 1st	Al Keen	l.pts.8	Cardiff

13

John Gamble

John Gamble was born in Merthyr on December 18th, 1942. He took up boxing in 1953 and as a youngster he reached the finals of the Schoolboy Championships. He then began to make his mark in the Army Cadet Championships, but in truth, he was an all-round sportsman. He had been tipped as a schoolboy soccer international and impressed in a trial with West Bromwich Albion, but he was also a useful cricketer. However, by about the age of sixteen he had matured into a talented southpaw and became one of the most successful members of Dowlais ABC.

In May 1958 he represented Wales in a Schoolboy International at the Colston Hall in Bristol against England and so impressed the selectors that he was chosen to represent Wales against Ireland at Cardiff in May, where he beat A. Twomey on points, having floored his opponent in the second round.

I had the good fortune to see John box at Dowlais Central School, the Hoover Factory Restaurant, the Miners' Hall in Merthyr and at Cefn Coed and it was clear that he was an exciting puncher.

At the age of seventeen, he made a brilliant start to his senior career beating Derek Jones of the Amman Valley Club on points. Jones was nine years older than John and even though both boxers went down during the contest, Gamble clinched the verdict with an overwhelming last round. This contest was part of the Welsh ABA's annual Boxing Day tournament held at the Drill Hall in Dumfries Place, Cardiff, and John became the first holder of a trophy awarded by the BBC for the best performance of the day.

One of the big names that appears on the amateur record of John Gamble is that of Vic Andrietti who boxed for the Fitzroy Lodge Club. As a professional he would go on to win the British Junior Welterweight title as it was then known, but he was conceding six pounds in weight to John and suffered his first defeat in four years. Even though Andrietti was regarded as a puncher, he could not cope with the variety and power of John's work.

Along with Don James and Dai Harris, John became National Coal Board Champion in 1960, beating Fred Powney on points at St. Andrew's Hall, Glasgow, thus providing the stable with a hat-trick of champions when this was a prestigious title. Another of the NCB champions that year was Jack Bodell, who went on to become British Heavyweight Champion. Johnny worked underground for a time at Eddie's mine but soon went to work at Hancock's Brewery in Merthyr alongside Howard Winstone.

On April 1st, 1961, John won the Welsh ABA title outpointing Derek Richards to win the title in Cardiff. The fight was closely contested and John was shaken on a couple of occasions but Gamble put everything into the last round and clinched the decision, much to Richards' annoyance. Richards, at 6ft 2ins held advantages in both height and reach but Gamble stuck manfully to his task to take the title. The name of Derek Richards appears elsewhere in this book as he was to cause problems for future stablemates Eddie Avoth and Stuart Price.

Following in the footsteps of Howard Winstone, John was now to become the second British ABA Champion to come out of Dowlais ABC. At the ABA Finals at Wembley on April 28th, John outpointed English international Brian Gale in the semi-final and knocked out Scottish international Bob Keddie in the third round to win the Lightmiddleweight title. Victory came with just 42 seconds of the contest remaining and fellow champions included Walter McGowan at Flyweight, Jack Bodell at Lightheavyweight and Billy Walker at Heavyweight. Soon afterwards Welsh ABA officials tried to persuade John to enter the European Championships, where it was thought that he would certainly be amongst the medals, but in a short time it was announced that he would be turning professional with his long-time mentor, Eddie Thomas, who felt that he would surely achieve his potential in the professional ring and become champion at Middleweight following fellow-Welshmen Tom Thomas and Frank Moody.

John had represented Wales at international level but it is an interesting statistic that Gerald Jones, Gordon Davies, John Gamble and Stuart Price all won Welsh ABA titles in 1961 while Glyn Davies was runner-up in the bantamweight division. All five would come under the wing of Eddie Thomas as professionals, but they all entered the paid ranks with a solid background in the amateur game.

John made his professional debut in the plush surroundings of the National Sporting Club on June 26th, 1961 and began impressively by stopping Ken Chadwick of Bournemouth in the second round. John enjoyed a weight advantage of three and a half pounds over his more experienced opponent and there was little between them at the end of the first round. In the second round John caught Chadwick near the ropes and floored his opponent with a terrific left to the body.

Chadwick was up at nine but after another burst of punches to both head and body he was rescued by referee Harry Gibbs. This was one of Gibbs' early contests and he went on to become one of our finest referees. I had the pleasure of refereeing with him on a few occasions, but one in particular stands out.

In November 1985 he refereed a Commonwealth Heavyweight title eliminator in Splott between British Champion Trevor Hughroy Currie and an African fighter called Proud Kilimanjaro. I went with Harry to the visiting fighter's dressing room and listened as he explained our rules rapidly in his Cockney accent. I am convinced that Kilimanjaro did not understand a single word. The contest was awful to watch but Currie was well ahead by the end of the eighth round. Gibbs then went to the African's corner and only later did I discover exactly what was said. Gibbs said "You haven't come all this way to fight like that for me son, have you? I think you can do better than that!"

Throughout rounds nine and ten Kilimanjaro punched Currie all round the ring and at the final bell Harry promptly raised Currie's hand. He was certainly one of boxing's great characters.

Following a points win over Allan Kaihau at Liverpool John was matched with Dave George at Wembley on December 5th. This was on the undercard of the contest between Zora Folley and Henry Cooper. Unfortunately, Henry was knocked out in the second round and John was disqualified in the third. He ended the year topping the bill at the Miners' Hall in Merthyr on December 19th, stopping Joe Somerville in the second round. This was a good result because Joe was an experienced performer. The referee was Ike Powell, who described Somerville's task in his Daily Express column as "a hopeless quest". Merthyr Express reporter "Jason" enthused:"The Merthyr southpaw looked a cut above Somerville from the first bell and a right hook sent the Englishman down for seven in round one." John went after his man again in the second round and floored Somerville once more before Ike uttered his familiar expression,"That's enough."

He opened 1962 by stopping John West in the second round at the Royal Albert Hall on a bill topped by Howard Winstone defeating Oripes Dos Santos on points and John notched up a further six wins in Wales on bills featuring Winstone and other members of the stable. Against West, the power of John's punching was again very much in evidence and he floored the Brighton man for three long counts in the second round before the referee decided he had seen enough. His performance earned the following tribute from journalist Sid Bailey, who wrote:" Gamble's perfectly timed counter-punching was a delight to watch. Here is a future British champion if ever I saw one." Another, impressed by this performance was the doyen of British boxing writers at the time, the legendary Peter Wilson. He felt that John's hand speed, power and all-round variety would take him a long way.

On January 29th he beat Kid Solomon, an awkward opponent, on points over six rounds in Cardiff and in February he stopped Bob Roberts in the seventh round at the Miners' Hall in Merthyr in what would have been his first eight-round contest. Stoppage wins followed over Steve Richards, Ivor Evans at Cardiff, Gordon White at the Parc and Dare Hall in Treorchy and he then knocked out Ron Vale at the Market Hall in Carmarthen.

The contest against Gordon White took place on June 22nd, 1962 and was John's tenth professional engagement. White, from London, had beaten Cardiff's Johnny Furnham in two rounds and was regarded as a puncher, but John floored White with a right hand early in the first round and he was down a couple more times before the bell sounded to end the round, at which point Gordon returned shakily to his corner. At the start of the second round White attempted to keep the contest at long range but was brushed aside and floored again. When he rose, John continued to pile on the pressure and the referee stepped between them at 1 min 41 secs of the round.

It was a performance characterised by power which drew comparison with that of Randolph Turpin from Alan Wood, writing in the "Western Mail", but Eddie Thomas was a little concerned that the quick endings were not providing John with the necessary experience and there was a feeling that John was running out of suitable opponents.

Already, Eddie was under pressure to match John with Phil Edwards, the Welsh Middleweight Champion, but he was in no mood to rush his young protégé. However, the hand speed and power John showed in knocking out Ronnie Vale in his next contest was almost enough to make Thomas re-think his strategy.

His final contest of the year came on August 2nd at Sophia Gardens Pavilion, Cardiff when Howard beat Dennis Adjei. John was matched with Fitzroy Lindo who was a tough, durable opponent. The contest was stopped in the seventh round with John having sustained a horrific gash above his left eye.

Since Eddie was involved in the promotion I had been selling programmes again that night and ended up in the dressing room straight after the fight. I had never before seen a boxing injury being stitched and this was a first for me. The doctor on duty was Dr Sammy Bloom from Merthyr, our old family doctor, whose reputation as a surgeon was legendary, but I shall never forget the sight of the flesh being pulled together as the doctor went about his work. It was something which has stayed in my mind to this day and still influences my thinking when I have to stop a contest because of an eye injury. Eddie felt that John was sustaining cuts so frequently that an operation to remove scar tissue would help and John was subsequently out of the ring until January, 1963 when he returned to the National Sporting Club and beat Joe Bell on a fourth round disqualification.

A little over a month later he was in action again, this time at the Royal Albert Hall when Brian Curvis stopped Tony Smith in defence of his British and Empire titles. Unfortunately, John was stopped in the first round by Teddy Haynes in what was to be his last contest in Britain. This was a bad knockout and its visible effects troubled Eddie Thomas greatly, so much so that he insisted that John should retire from boxing.

He had been detained overnight for observation at St. George's Hospital in London but was released the next day with no apparent ill-effects. But when Eddie arrived at the hospital to visit John he immediately said that John would not be boxing again. John himself was bewildered by this hasty decision and it left him with a feeling of bitterness which he retains to this day. John would have welcomed a short break followed by a return to the gym with a rational decision concerning his future taken in the course of time, but it seems that Eddie's mind was already made up.

The words of Eddie Thomas loomed large in the minds of John and his family, who were now having to contemplate a future without boxing. In an interview with a Daily Express reporter, John's mother told of how he would be heartbroken if he were forced to retire. John was the family breadwinner and she compared his ring earnings with those as a £9 per week brewery worker. She also told of how John had paid out over £100 to enable his sister to train as a hairdresser, but there was a glimmer of hope on March 31st, 1963, when Dr Huw Walters, honorary medical officer to the Welsh Area Council of the British Boxing Board of Control pronounced John fit to return to boxing but added that the opinion of a consultant would be sought.

The appropriate X-rays were taken and there did appear to be a shadow, but the medical people were unable to ascertain whether or not this was boxing related or congenital. Ironically, shortly before she died in 2003, John's mother underwent an X-ray which revealed a similar shadow. Had our present day sophisticated brain scans been available it is quite possible that John would have been allowed to continue his career as some boxers have been allowed with a rigorous monitoring and review process in place.

John found this period of uncertainty difficult to accept and with Eddie insisting on retirement, John contemplated joining Cardiff manager Benny Jacobs in an attempt to continue his career, but during this time it seems that the British Boxing Board of Control were prepared to overrule the Welsh Area Council in ensuring the boxer's well-being.

He continued to train but his career ground to a halt for two years and during this frustrating time John returned to his other love, soccer, and he signed for Merthyr Town. He played for them in a number of Welsh League matches but could not overcome his disappointment at not being able to box and eventually decided to go to Australia for a time in an attempt to resurrect his career.

John did manage to re-enter the ring in Australia and impressed journalist Merv

Williams with his performance in stopping Hans Waschewski in the sixth of a ten round contest at the Festival Hall in Melbourne. Williams was impressed with John's destructive southpaw style. He wrote:"He's well balanced, looks where he's punching and hurts with either hand. He could give the 11.6 class a shot in the arm."

Sadly for John the British Boxing Board of Control eventually got to hear of his return to the ring, undoubtedly, in his opinion, prompted by Eddie Thomas. The Board in turn contacted the Australian Boxing Federation, who upheld the ban and John had to accept that his ring career was over, but he has continued his involvement in the game by becoming a successful trainer, working closely with former stablemate Gerald Jones.

He was awarded his Welsh ABA Coaching Certificate in March 1973 and has worked with a steady stream of champions. His most recent success was with David Davies of Merthyr who became Welsh ABA Featherweight Champion in 2004 and who has now turned professional but John will continue to be involved in his career.

It seems so unfortunate that the career of this hugely talented, flame-haired southpaw was over in such a short space of time. Boxing, by its very nature is the toughest of sports and the ring is without doubt the most unforgiving of places. John was tipped as a future champion by so many experts and he boxed in the most exciting of divisions. I feel sure he would have enhanced the great traditions of the middleweight division, but cruelly, he was deprived of the opportunity. Forty years on, and without seeing the medical records of the time, it is difficult to be absolutely certain, but I have the impression that the career of John Gamble came to an end on the strength of gut feeling and instinct ahead of specific medical evidence.

John Gamble

Born: Merthyr Tydfil Dec 18th, 1942
1959/60 NCB Champion
1961 Welsh ABA and ABA Lightmiddleweight Champion
Welsh International

Professional Record

1961

Jun 26th	Ken Chadwick	w.rsf.2	London
Aug 24th	Allan Kaihau	w.pts.6	Liverpool
Dec 5th	Dave George	l.dis.3	Wembley
Dec 19th	Joe Sommerville	w.rsf.2	Merthyr

1962

Jan 9th	John West	w.rsf.2	London
Jan 29th	Kid Solomon	w.pts.6	Cardiff
Feb 26th	Bob Roberts	w.rtd.7	Merthyr
May 8th	Steve Richards	w.rtd.5	Treorchy

1962 cont

May 30th	Ivor Evans	w.rsf.2	Cardiff
Jun 22nd	Gordon White	w.rsf.2	Treorchy
Jul 9th	Ron Vale	w.ko.5	Carmarthen
Aug 2nd	Fitzroy Lindo	l.rsf.7	Cardiff

1963

| Jan 7th | Joe Bell | w.dis.4 | London |
| Feb 12th | Teddy Haynes | l.rsf.1 | London |

*After moving to Australia, John engaged in one further contest:

| Hans Waschewski | w.rsc.6 | Festival Hall | Melbourne |

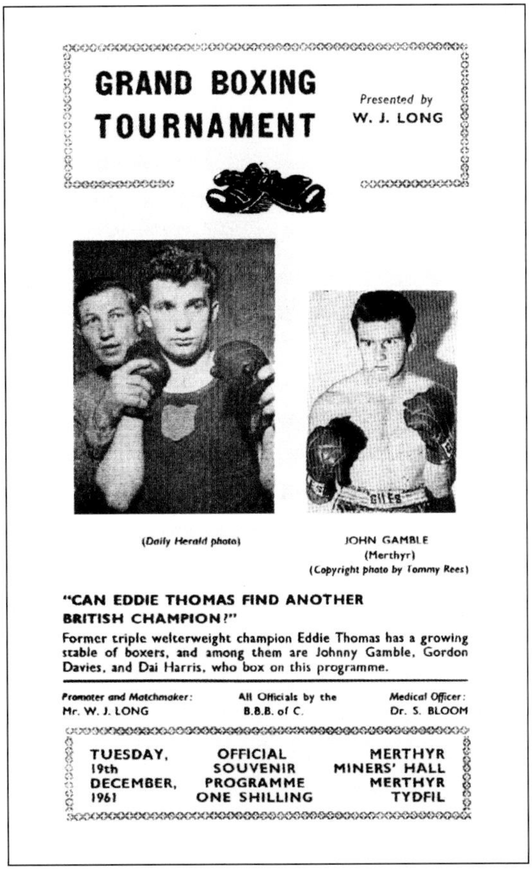

GRAND BOXING TOURNAMENT
Presented by W. J. LONG

(Daily Herald photo)   JOHN GAMBLE
(Merthyr)
(Copyright photo by Tommy Rees)

"CAN EDDIE THOMAS FIND ANOTHER BRITISH CHAMPION?"
Former triple welterweight champion Eddie Thomas has a growing stable of boxers, and among them are Johnny Gamble, Gordon Davies, and Dai Harris, who box on this programme.

Promoter and Matchmaker: Mr. W. J. LONG
All Officials by the B.B.B. of C.
Medical Officer: Dr. S. BLOOM

TUESDAY, 19th DECEMBER, 1961
OFFICIAL SOUVENIR PROGRAMME
ONE SHILLING
MERTHYR MINERS' HALL MERTHYR TYDFIL

JOHN GAMBLE

14

Don James

On December 31st, 2003 Don James celebrated his sixtyfifth birthday and retirement from his post in the National Health Service. To mark the occasion, Don's wife Lillian had arranged a surprise party at the Bessemer Hotel in Dowlais and I was brought in to introduce a "This Is Your Life" style presentation. It was an emotional night, with Don's son, daughter in law and grandson having returned from Australia especially for the celebrations, but boxing provided perhaps the most significant element throughout the evening, reflecting its importance to Don.

He was born in Merthyr Tydfil in 1938 and started boxing at the age of ten. He trained at the gym of Billy Evans along with Howard Winstone and the pair were to remain lifelong friends. They went to Queens Road school together and boxed on many of the same shows. When their gym at the Labour Club was closed the boys were forced to travel to Cilfynydd and made the trip, along with Ken Jones and Alan Stephens, three times a week. Eventually, this arrangement began to take its toll and Don and Howard eventually walked up the steps of the Old Snooker Hall in High Street, Penydarren to join the Dowlais Amateur Boxing Club. Don tells a story of having to get past the figure of Billy Long, Eddie's great friend and assistant, and of Billy making a jocular comment to Eddie about the arrival of two future champions! I wonder if Billy ever thought about the prophetic nature of that remark during the years of success that were to follow?

I remember seeing them both box on a show at Dowlais Central School in March, 1958 along with stablemates Johnny Gamble and Billy Gardner, but Don and Howard were to spar many rounds together and to cover many miles of roadwork together over the years. In later years Howard acknowledged Don's help and quality as a sparring partner because this could be a soul destroying task for many boxers when Winstone was at his peak. When Howard began to find his way back into boxing following the horrific factory accident which deprived him of the tips of three fingers on his right hand, he and Don would use an old punch bag rigged up in a pig sty on a small holding owned by Howard's father. They also adapted a right glove for Howard and the man who had previously enjoyed a tear-up developed one of the finest left hands ever seen in British boxing.

In an amateur career that extended to over 300 contests there were titles galore and numerous international vests, though he once missed out on a trip to Switzerland by having to bring forward his wedding day because Lillian's father was terminally ill.

His decision to opt out of the trip meant that he was then overlooked for a time by the Welsh selectors, but he was eventually brought in from the cold. He remembers with pride and affection his epic battles with Brian Hungerford which would fill any venue. On the title front, Don won a Welsh ABA Youth title and in 1960 he won both the National Coal Board Championship at flyweight and he also won the Welsh ABA Flyweight Championship whilst working at Merthyr Vale Colliery.

During his last few months as an amateur Don represented Wales against Denmark in Cardiff, losing on points to Villy Andersen on January 22nd, 1960, but his international career ended on a high note with a points win over H. Wijholds of Holland at the Grand Pavilion, Porthcawl on March 3rd.

One of his most significant wins came against the Scot Bobby Mallon, who went on to win the Gold Medal at Flyweight in the 1962 Commonwealth Games in Perth, Australia, but undoubtedly, Don's biggest win as an amateur came against another Scot, namely Walter McGowan. Walter went on to become an exceptional British champion and later became Flyweight Champion of the World when he took the title from Italy's Salvatore Burruni. They had been due to meet at the Miners' Hall in Merthyr, but eventually boxed at RAF St Athan.

Don turned professional with Eddie Thomas and made his debut on June 23rd, 1960 at Birmingham. He made a good start, outpointing the experienced Barry Adgie over six rounds. Adgie was an extremely busy flyweight and he was again the opponent in Don's second contest which took place on August 15th at Aberdare with Don repeating his points victory. This was on the undercard of the contest between British Flyweight Champion Frankie Jones against Ron "Ponty" Davies of Llanbradach, with Jones winning on points over ten rounds, while on the same bill, Howard Winstone stopped Sergio Milan in the sixth round.

Next up was Billy Colvin on September 22nd in Cardiff on a bill which featured former British and Empire Heavyweight Champion Joe Erskine, Howard Winstone, Ron "Ponty" Davies and Terry Crimmins, the bantamweight from Cardiff. Colvin was from Belfast and was an experienced performer but was beaten by Don on points over the six round course. They met for a second time on December 28th at the National Sporting Club and Colvin was stopped in the fourth round giving Don an unblemished record as the year ended.

Unfortunately, the successes did not last into 1961. On January 19th, he was forced to retire in three rounds against another Belfast man, Alex O'Neill. Don returned to the National Sporting Club on May 29th and lost on points over six rounds to old foe Billy Colvin in what was their third encounter and then, on June 12th he was stopped in the second round by Danny Lee, again at the NSC. Don was already beginning to feel the pressures of having a young family and was still employed at Merthyr Vale Colliery. He arrived for the weigh-in at the Club and was a pound and a half overweight. He refused to attempt to remove the excess weight but had to starve himself up to fight time. Danny Lee was a good fighter and in 1960 won the ABA Flyweight Championship. He went through 1961 undefeated, beating the likes of Danny Wells and Don Braithwaite while in 1962 he lost to Walter McGowan and Alex O'Neill, another of Don's former opponents, so the stoppage, on a cut, was no disgrace.

After the Lee contest, opportunities seemed to dry up for Don. Contests were promised but never materialised and had John Gamble been allowed to continue his career under the guidance of Benny Jacobs, Don, too, may have made the switch in an attempt to resurrect his career. As it was, Gerald Jones was making good progress and Glyn Davies joined the stable. Don tells the story of how he was asked by Eddie to give Glyn a couple of rounds on his first night at the gym. Don was under instruction to take it easy, but began to enjoy the session and started to expose one or two weaknesses in the young fighter, much to the frustration and anger of Eddie, but much to the amusement of Howard Winstone, who was skipping, ringside, and who gave Don a knowing wink.

Don eventually decided to retire but set up a boxing club at the Hoover Factory in Merthyr when he went to work there. It was here that he began to work with the young Johnny Owen and to transform his boxing style because Johnny's physique did not really allow him to be an out and out fighter.

Don eventually took out a professional manager's licence and his first signing was Martyn Galleozzie but the partnership was shortlived with Don maintaining that Martyn should not have accepted the contest with Vernon Sollas, who knocked him out in the seventh round of their contest in London. Galleozzie then moved on to Cardiff manager Mac Williams and will always be remembered for his epic battles with fellow Merthyr fighter Johnny Wall.

Don meanwhile, continued to assemble a stable of fighters which included Allan Jones, Charlie Quist, Howard Williams, Roy Williams, Mike Wilkes, Colin Neagle and Steve James. He also took on David Miles and Roger Barlow when their contracts with Eddie Thomas expired. I had the pleasure of refereeing some of these boxers at venues such as the Club Double Diamond in Caerphilly, the Afan Lido in Aberavon and Rhydycar Leisure Centre in Merthyr, and it is always good to meet them again having played a small part in their careers.

In more recent years Don has been the driving force behind the Welsh Ex-Boxers' Association, playing a key role as secretary. He was the man who ensured that the statue erected in memory of his lifelong friend, Howard Winstone became a reality and he also served on the committee of the Johnny Owen Memorial Appeal Fund where his experience was invaluable. He enjoys visiting other Ex-Boxers' Associations and for several years has been leading groups to Canastota for the International Boxing Hall of Fame Induction Weekend.

Don James

Born: Merthyr Tydfil Dec 31st, 1938
Welsh ABA Youth Title
NCBABA Champion 1959/60
Welsh ABA Flyweight Champion 1960
Welsh International

Professional Record

1960

Jun 23rd	Barry Adgie	w.pts.6	Birmingham
Aug 15th	Barry Adgie	w.pts.6	Aberdare
Sep 22nd	Billy Colvin	w.pts.6	Cardiff
Dec 28th	Billy Colvin	w.rsf.4	London

1961

Jan 19th	Alex O'Neill	l.rtd.3	Cardiff
May 29th	Billy Colvin	l.pts.6	London
Jun 12th	Danny Lee	l.rsf.2	London

NATIONAL SPORTING CLUB

BOXING TOURNAMENT

LADIES NIGHT

Monday, May 29th, 1961

PROGRAMME

Bout 1
8 (3) Minute Rounds Bantamweight Contest at 8 stone 9 lbs
TERRY CRIMMINS v JOHNNY O'CALLAGHAN
(Cardiff)   (Dagenham)
No. 1 Contender for Welsh
Area Title.

Bout 2
6 (3) Minute Rounds Lightweight Contest at 9 stone 12 lbs
TEDDY CARTER v SAMMY McSPADDEN
(Middlesborough)   (Fulham)

Bout 3
6 (3) Minute Rounds Bantamweight Contest at 8 stone 8 lbs
DANNY WELLS v DAI CORP
(Basildon)   (Cardiff)

Bout 4
6 (3) Minute Rounds Flyweight Contest at 8 stone 3 lbs
DON JAMES v BILLY COLVIN
(Dowlais)   (Peckham)

Next Tournament - Monday, June 12th, 1961.

Stuart Price

Stuart Price was born at Cymmer Afan on November 20th, 1941. He was a very successful amateur boxer who represented Wales several times and in 1961 he won the Welsh ABA Middleweight Championship, outpointing T. Howe to take the decision.

He took part in Wales' 6-4 win against Luxembourg at Port Talbot Drill Hall when John Gamble made such an impression in stopping Franco Sabadini in what was his international debut. Stuart followed Gamble's win by outpointing Luxembourg Champion Emile Phillipe, using his height and reach cleverly to secure the decision.

When he boxed for Wales against Belgium on May 11th, 1961, his team mates included Gerald Jones, Glyn Davies and Gordon Davies, all of whom would become stablemates under the guidance of Eddie Thomas. They were all successful, with Stuart stopping A. Marlett in the third round and Wales winning by seven bouts to three. When he beat Bob Boulwizan in the international against Holland at the Hoover Factory, Pentrebach on October 26th Malcolm Price was one of his team mates, as was future opponent Derek Richards.

Stuart, a tall rangy southpaw, made his professional debut on February 12th, 1962 at Maesteg and beat Roy Seward on points over six rounds. His next contest was at Wembley on April 10th, when he stopped Peter Russell in the fourth round. This was the night when Howard Winstone stopped Derry Treanor in the fourteenth round to retain his British title and on the same bill, the American Guy Sumlin stopped Brian Curvis in the eighth round.

On May 8th he beat Dave Wakefield of Hackney at the Parc and Dare Hall, Treorchy. Weighing in at 11st 8 lbs he punished Wakefield severely and with Wakefield having sustained damage to his nose he was retired by his corner at the end of the third round.

Stuart notched up another five wins at various venues around Wales including a stoppage win over Joe Somerville, another tall southpaw, at Treorchy. Stuart dominated the contest, with Somerville spending most of the time on the receiving end of the Welshman's right glove and he ended the year by stopping Johnny West in the fifth round at the National Sporting Club.

He boxed only three times in 1963 stopping Maurice Loughran in the first round in Cardiff on the undercard of Howard Winstone's win over the Frenchman Gracieux

Lamperti. He lost his next contest against Johnny Angel on points over eight rounds at Bangor but in July, he was back at the National Sporting Club beating Tommy Baldwin on points.

There were only two contests in 1964 and these were both defeats, with the contests only three weeks apart. On July 6th he was stopped in the fourth round by Clarence Prince at the National Sporting Club and on July 28th, on the Brian Curvis/Johnny Cooke bill at Coney Beach Arena, Porthcawl he retired after seven rounds against Derek Richards in a contest for the Welsh Lightheavyweight title. Two years later Derek went on to beat Eddie Avoth in another contest for the Welsh title, this time winning on points over ten rounds. They were both gruelling battles and the stablemates both experienced the same problems with Richards. Derek was a good amateur boxer who became Welsh Middleweight Champion in 1962 and he was always a tough, awkward opponent in the professional ring as his wins over Stuart and Eddie show.

Sadly, the defeat against Richards marked the end of Stuart's career but he has continued his involvement in the amateur game as a successful trainer.

Stuart Price

Born: Cymmer Afan Nov 20th, 1941
Welsh ABA Middleweight Champion 1961
Welsh International

Professional Record

1962

Feb 12th	Roy Seward	w.pts.6	Maesteg
Apr 10th	Peter Russell	w.rsf.4	Wembley
May 8th	Dave Wakefield	w.rtd.3	Treorchy
Jun 22nd	Joe Sommerville	w.rsf.4	Treorchy
Jul 9th	Herbie Williams	w.rsf.2	Carmarthen
Aug 18th	Julius Caesar	w.pts.8	Newtown
Nov 12th	Joe Bell	w.pts.8	Aberdare
Nov 26th	Johnny West	w.rsf.5	London

1963

Apr 29th	Maurice Loughran	w.rtd.1	Cardiff
May 17th	Johnny Angel	l.pts.8	Bangor
Jul 1st	Tommy Baldwin	w.pts.8	London

1964

Jul 6th	Clarence Prince	l.rsf.4	London
Jul 28th	Derek Richards	l.rtd.7	Porthcawl

16

Gerry Banwell

Gerry Banwell was born in Tonyrefail on May 1st, 1942. He did not come to the professional ranks with the same kind of amateur pedigree as some of his more illustrious stablemates but I always looked forward to seeing him in the gym. To my mind, he was the resident comedian, though several of the others ran him close.

His career ran to nineteen contests with five defeats. He made his professional debut as a welterweight at Newtown on August 18th, 1962 beating Steve Ako on points over six rounds. He then lost his next contest at Liverpool, beaten on points by Jimmy Nicholls. Gerry then put together four wins, three of them coming on Eddie's promotional circuit.

He beat Gerry Maxwell, the tough former Welsh international from Caerphilly, who retired in four rounds at New Tredegar and followed up with wins over Steve Ellwood at Maesteg and Wally Williams at Aberdare, ending the year with a return against Ellwood at the National Sporting Club. This time, Ellwood was forced to retire after two rounds.

He lost his first contest of 1963 to Johnny Fuller at the NSC but was back in London eight days later to stop Jim Lloyd in three rounds at the Royal Albert Hall. This was on the night when stablemate John Gamble suffered a catastrophic defeat at the hands of Teddy Haynes. Fortunately, it was a different story for Gerry. Jim Lloyd was the ABA Lightmiddleweight Champion in 1962 and was an Olympic Games bronze medallist, so this result was quite an upset.

Gerry was working at Coed Ely Colliery when he received a call which meant a dash to London to substitute for Mickey Pearce of Hendon against Lloyd.

Eddie came in for criticism before the contest started with some experts claiming that Banwell had been overmatched, but Gerry startled Lloyd by flooring him with a long right in the first round. He was happy to trade punches in the next round and by the third round, Lloyd's eye was beginning to swell. He continued to put Lloyd under pressure and the referee was forced to intervene, much to the delight of the Welsh camp. He followed this up with four more wins but his last fight of the year came at Wembley on September 10th when he lost to Young Gabriel on points over six rounds. This was on the undercard of the first contest between Billy Walker and Johnny Prescott with Walker stopping Prescott in the tenth round with only 84 seconds of the contest remaining. Prescott's boxing skills looked to be winning the fight, but Walker began to unload in the last round and floored Prescott, who rose in time to beat the count, but the referee stopped the contest.

Another contest which featured on the bill was the eagerly awaited return between Frankie "The Tiger" Taylor and Lennie "The Lion" Williams, with Taylor having won their first encounter by knockout in the sixth round. Frankie Taylor was again the victor, but this time on a fourth round retirement. It seems incredible that this major Wembley promotion featured ten-rounders as the main attractions. Not a title fight to be seen, and yet it was a high quality card, which surely shows today's promoters and television companies that a title fight from one of the many sanctioning bodies is not an essential ingredient for a successful promotion. These were genuine, meaningful matches which would have sold out any arena.

Gerry's first contest of 1964 came in February at the NSC and he lost on points over eight rounds to Dave Wakefield, this time at the middleweight poundage. Three more wins followed and on July 28th, at Coney Beach Arena, Porthcawl he beat the Scot Willie Fisher on a seventh round disqualification. The bill was topped by Brian Curvis defending his British and Empire titles against Johnny Cooke, but also featured stablemates Stuart Price and Glyn Davies.

Gerry was then inactive for almost five months and on December 14th he faced Joe Bell at the National Sporting Club. He was stopped in the fifth round and that was his last contest.

All in all, the career of Gerry Banwell was comparatively short but he appeared on major London promotions, boxed seven times in Wales and appeared several times at the National Sporting Club, where so many of his stablemates also appeared with distinction.

Gerry was a hard man and a tough fighter, like so many from a mining background. Indeed, on more than one occasion, Eddie turned up at the pithead to inform Gerry at the end of his shift that he was boxing that evening, and so, after an exhausting day at the coal-face, off they would go to the venue in question. Sadly, he was not at the stable re-union and I know that over the years he has not enjoyed the best of health, with stomach problems proving to be a major worry, but I shall always remember the laughter he brought to the gym.

Gerry Banwell

Born: Tonyrefail May 1st, 1942
Welterweight

Professional Record

1962

Aug 18th	Steve Ako	w.pts.6	Newtown
Sep 6th	Jimmy Nicholls	l.pts.6	Liverpool
Sep 24th	Gerry Maxwell	w.rtd.4	New Tredegar
Oct 29th	Steve Elwood	w.pts.6	Maesteg
Nov 12th	Wally Williams	w.rsf.6	Aberdare
Nov 26th	Steve Elwood	w.rtd.2	London

1963

Feb 4th	Johnny Fuller	l.pts.6	London
Feb 12th	Jim Lloyd	w.rsf.3	London
Mar 20th	Eric Young	w.rsf.4	London
Jun 7th	Joe Falcon	w.pts.8	Cardiff
Jun 17th	Jack Burley	w.pts.8	London
Jul 9th	Jimmy Brown	w.pts.6	Cardiff
Sep 10th	Young Gabriel	l.pts.6	Wembley

1964

Feb 24th	Dave Wakefield	l.pts.8	London
Mar 16th	Billy Linton	w.pts.8	Manchester
May 19th	Tommy Hayes	w.rsf.5	Penarth
Jun 8th	Steve Richards	w.pts.8	London
Jul 28th	Willie Fisher	w.dis.7	Porthcawl
Dec 14th	Joe Bell	l.rsf.5	London

17

Roy John

Roy John was born in Abercynon, the birthplace of former British, Empire and European Flyweight Champion Dai Dower on October 13th, 1947 and enjoyed an extremely successful amateur career winning the Welsh ABA Lightheavyweight title in 1965, 66 and 67 and he also represented Wales many times at international level.

He made his professional debut on one of Welsh boxing's great nights appearing on the undercard of the second meeting between Howard Winstone and Vicente Saldivar at Ninian Park, Cardiff on June 15th, 1967. He beat Dervan Airey on points over six rounds and was back in action within a fortnight, making his first appearance at the National Sporting Club, but was unfortunately stopped in the sixth round by James Bevan.

A run of four wins followed, the first being against Jimmy Bryant who was stopped in the sixth round at Aberavon. The date was July 26th and topping the bill was Ken Buchanan against the Frenchman Rene Roque.

He then beat Clarence Cassius at the World Sporting Club run by Jack Solomons and repeated the win five weeks later at Brighton. He ended the year with a six rounds points win over Jack Powe on the undercard of the contest between Carl Gizzi and Hubert Hilton at Aberavon.

Roy boxed eight times in 1968 winning five on points and losing three, going the distance each time. On July 24th he beat Nojeen Adigun over eight rounds at Coney Beach Arena when Howard Winstone lost his World Featherweight title to Jose Legra.

After losing to Dick Duffy at the NSC in October, Roy faced Carl Thomas on November 27th in Cardiff for the Welsh Middleweight title and was outpointed over ten rounds.

Roy was then inactive until June 24th, 1969 when he beat Maxie Smith on points over eight rounds at the NSC, having decided that his future now lay in the lightheavyweight division. He then beat Jeff Shaw in Manchester but ended the year by losing to Lloyd Walford at the National Sporting Club.

During 1970, Roy boxed six times, winning three and losing three, boxing in Solihull, Manchester, London and Johannesburg where he was knocked out in the sixth round by Kosie Smith.

Roy opened 1971 with his third contest against Lloyd Walford and he was beaten on points. Walford was not a great fighter but he now led by two contests to one in their series. On March 16th Roy outpointed Phil Matthews at Wembley. This was on the night when Henry Cooper lost his British and Empire Heavyweight titles controversially to Joe Bugner on points over fifteen rounds. Henry had indicated that this would probably be his final contest. It had been closely contested and at the final bell, referee Harry Gibbs raised Bugner's arm in victory, but the British public never seemed to forgive Bugner for beating Britain's longest reigning Heavyweight Champion. Eddie was working as the cut-man in Cooper's corner that night for the third time following the departure of Danny Holland, who had been with Henry for many years.

Phil Matthews linked up with Eddie for a time and developed a reputation as a puncher, but lost in his challenge against Bunny Sterling for the British Middleweight title. The contest took place in Manchester on September 19th, 1972 and Matthews was knocked out in the fifth round. This defeat came as a bitter shock to Phil, who, in his previous contest had stopped the highly rated American Tom Bethea in three rounds in London.

Roy followed his win over Matthews with victories over Guinea Roger, and over Arno Prick on points over ten rounds in Johannesburg, but he ended the year with defeats in Milan and Bologna. He had obviously reached the stage where he was prepared to travel and accepted contests which were more likely to earn good money than to yield favourable results, but in 1972, after a win in Charleville and a points defeat in Rotterdam he beat Johnny Frankham on points over twelve rounds in an eliminator for the British Lightheavyweight title. Frankham was the fancied fighter and many thought the result to be a foregone conclusion, but Roy came out on top in the televised contest giving a superb display of rugged aggression to take the decision.

By now, Roy was being looked after by Bobby Neill, the former British Featherweight Champion, but Roy did not want to move to London and continued to train at the gym in Penydarren under the watchful eye of Howard Winstone.

He then had to wait five months for his shot at the title and this came on March 13th, 1973 at Wembley when he was beaten on points over fifteen rounds by Chris Finnegan, the man who had taken this very title from stablemate Eddie Avoth. This was a gruelling battle and Roy did not return to the ring until November, when he was beaten by Tom Bogs in Copenhagen. Three weeks later, he was back in action in Cardiff, losing on points to previous victim, Maxie Smith.

Reflecting on the contest with Finnegan, Roy still feels a sense of frustration. This was a contest he feels he should have won. He was paid £3,000 for this contest and at the weigh-in, promoter Mickey Duff offered Roy £15,000 to defend his title against John Conteh should he emerge as the winner. This was a substantial sum of money at the time and one can understand Roy's sense of frustration at what might have been.

Roy's career was now losing direction and he was inactive during 1974. He returned to the ring in 1975, by which time he had linked up with promoter Bev Walker, and his third fight of the year was against Bob Tuckett at the Club Double Diamond in Caerphilly. By now, I had moved back to Wales from the Leeds area where I had started out on my scoring tests in the quest for a referee's licence.

My tests now had to continue under the Welsh Area Council and Roy's contest with Tuckett was one of my first scoring tests after returning home. Roy won on points over eight rounds and there were two more wins at Caerphilly before the end of the year. His final contest, on November 12th ended in a points win over twelve rounds against Tim Wood in an eliminator for the British Lightheavyweight title. He was very much back in title contention but was ruled out because of an eye injury and the opportunity to box for the vacant title fell to Tim Wood. Ironically, after winning the Lonsdale Belt outright by regaining his title from Johnny Frankham, Chris Finnegan was forced to retire from boxing with a detached retina, and the doors consequently opened for Wood and Phil Martin.

Tim Wood went on to beat Phil Martin on points over fifteen rounds to become British Lightheavyweight Champion on April 28th, 1976 at the World Sporting Club.

Roy John had been sidelined for many months with an eye-muscle problem but by June 1976 he had been given the all-clear to resume boxing and there was talk of a contest with Phil Martin. This contest did not materialise and Martin was matched with Bunny Johnson in a final eliminator on December 14th, at West Bromwich. Martin was stopped in the tenth round, but this meant that Roy went through 1976 without a contest.

Roy eventually returned to the ring on June 16th, 1977 at Ebbw Vale and beat George Gray on points over eight rounds at the Leisure Centre. In October he drew with Eddie Fenton over eight rounds at Kingston, but things had moved on and Roy now had to re-establish his credentials.

He was back in action on January 7th, 1978 when he took on Mustapha Wassaja at Randers, but after being stopped in the fifth round, decided to retire from boxing.

Roy's career ran to fortythree contests with twentyfive wins, seventeen losses and a draw. The names of Clarence Cassius and Lloyd Walford appear three and four times respectively on his record, and he could have been forgiven for thinking that at times, his career was going round in circles, but he seized his opportunity in style in his title eliminator with Johnny Frankham and clearly threw down the gauntlet. With a little luck against Chris Finnegan, things could have been so different, and his victory over Tim Wood late in 1975 showed that he was still a force to be reckoned with, only to be thwarted finally by injury.

Roy has always been a genial character, always able to take the rough with the smooth, and perhaps, in professional boxing, that is the best way to be.

Roy John

Born: Abercynon, October 13th, 1947
Welsh ABA Lightheavyweight Champion, 1965, 66 and 67
Welsh International

Professional Record

1967
Jun 15th	Dervan Airey	w.pts.6	Cardiff
Jun 28th	James Bevan	l.rsf.6	London
Jul 26th	Jimmy Bryant	w.rsf.6	Aberavon
Sep 14th	Clarence Cassius	w.pts.6	London
Oct 22nd	Clarence Cassius	w.pts.6	Brighton
Nov 28th	Jack Powe	w.pts.6	Aberavon

1968
Feb 7th	Clarence Cassius	l.pts.8	Merthyr
Apr 8th	Larry Brown	w.pts.8	London
Apr 24th	Tom Bell	w.pts.8	Cardiff
May 27th	Ernie Musso	w.pts.8	London
Jun 25th	Tom Bell	w.pts.8	London
Jul 24th	Nojeen Adigun	w.pts.8	Porthcawl
Oct 28th	Dick Duffy	l.pts.8	London
Nov 27th	Carl Thomas	l.pts.10	Cardiff
(Welsh Middleweight Title)			

1969
Jun 24th	Maxie Smith	w.pts.8	London
Sep 22nd	Jeff Shaw	w.pts.8	Manchester
Dec 15th	Lloyd Walford	l.pts.8	London

1970
Mar 4th	Dave Hawkes	w.rsf.7	Solihull
Mar 23rd	Lloyd Walford	l.pts.8	Manchester
Apr 23rd	Ray Brittle	l.dis.4	London
Aug 15th	Kosie Smith	l.ko.6	Johannesburg
Oct 12th	Lloyd Walford	w.rsf.8	London
Nov 11th	Guinea Roger	w.rsf.7	Solihull

1971
Jan 11th	Lloyd Walford	l.pts.8	London
Mar 16th	Phil Matthews	w.pts.8	Wembley
May 24th	Guinea Roger	w.pts.8	London
Sep 11th	Arno Prick	w.pts.10	Johannesburg
Oct 21st	Gianfranco Macchia	l.pts.10	Milan
Nov 28th	Domenico Adinolfi	l.pts.8	Bologna

1972
Jan 8th	Christian Poncelet	w.rtd.3	Charleville
Sep 25th	Bas van Duivenbode	l.pts.8	Rotterdam
Oct 24th	Johnny Frankham	w.pts.12	London
(Final elim British Lightheavyweight Title)			

1973
Mar 13th	Chris Finnegan	l.pts.15	Wembley
(British and Commonwealth Lightheavyweight titles)			
Nov 1st	Tom Bogs	l.pts.10	Copenhagen
Nov 21st	Maxie Smith	l.pts.8	Cardiff

1974
Inactive

1975
Jan 20th	George Gray	w.pts.8	London
Feb 10th	Bob Tuckett	l.dis.5	London
Apr 2nd	Bob Tuckett	w.pts.8	Caerphilly
Sep 29th	Jean-Claude Capitolin	w.pts.8	Caerphilly
Nov 12th	Tim Wood	w.pts.12	Caerphilly
(Final elim British Lightheavyweight title)			

1976
Inactive

1977
Jun 16th	George Gray	w.pts.8	Ebbw Vale
Oct 19th	Eddie Fenton	d.8	Kingston

1978
Jan 7th	Mustapha Wassaja	l.rsf.5	Randers

Roy John v Jean-Claude Capitolin (courtesy Roy John's personal collection)

18

Allan Ball

Allan Ball was born on September 24th, 1947 and came from Bargoed. He enjoyed an extremely successful amateur career, firstly winning junior titles, and then in 1965 he outpointed Clive Cook to win the Welsh ABA Middleweight title.

Clive Cook turned the tables on Allan in 1966, but in 1967, Allan was Welsh ABA Champion once more and on May 5th, he claimed the ABA title beating Chris Finnegan on points. In the same tournament, Roy John lost to Dickie Owens of Reading in the Lightheavyweight semi-final while Cardiff's Steve Curtis took the ABA Flyweight title.

Allan Ball also represented Wales at international level, and what with his championship record, great things were expected of him when he turned professional.

He made his debut on November 28th, 1967 at the Afan Lido, Aberavon when Carl Gizzi topped the bill against the American, Hubert Hilton. Allan stopped Lou Samuels in the fourth round but did not box again until March, 1968 when he forced Frank Poleon to retire in the second round at London's Anglo American Sporting Club.

On May 6th, he beat Sean Dolan on points at the National Sporting Club and was back there again in June when he knocked out Tony Monaghan in the fifth round. July was a busy month and on the 10th, he appeared at the World Sporting Club, where he stopped Steve Richards in the fifth round while nine days later he appeared at the Coney Beach Arena, Porthcawl stopping Chris Cox in the third round on the undercard of Howard Winstone's ill-fated title defence against Jose Legra. Stablemates Eddie Avoth, Roy John and Tony Williams were all in action on the same bill.

Allan's first setback came on November 4th, when he lost on points over eight rounds to Dickie Owens at Reading and on November 27th, he was stopped in the third round by Frank Poleon at Sophia Gardens, Cardiff. Top of the bill was Carl Gizzi against Jack Bodell in a final eliminator for Henry Cooper's British, Empire and European Heavyweight titles. It turned out to be a poor night for the stable with Gizzi being stopped in two rounds and Roy John also losing to Carl Thomas in a contest for the vacant Middleweight Championship of Wales.

Allan was subsequently out of the ring for a year and returned against Maxie Smith at Bermondsey on November 26th, 1969, losing on points over eight rounds. His next contest came on March 23rd, 1970 against Ray Brittle at the World Sporting Club and Allan was disqualified in the fifth round. This was now his fourth successive defeat and Allan decided to retire from boxing, sadly, without realising to the full the potential he had shown during his amateur career.

Allan Ball

Born: Bargoed, September 24th, 1947
Welsh ABA Middleweight Champion, 1965, 1967
ABA Middleweight Champion, 1967
Welsh International

Professional Record

1967

Nov 28th	Lou Samuels	w.rsf.4	Aberavon

1968

Mar 11th	Frank Poleon	w.rtd.2	London
May 6th	Sean Dolan	w.pts.6	London
Jun 10th	Tony Monaghan	w.ko.5	London
Jul 15th	Steve Richards	w.rsf.5	London
Jul 24th	Chris Cox	w.rsf.3	Porthcawl
Nov 4th	Dickie Owens	l.pts.8	Reading
Nov 27th	Frank Poleon	l.rsf.3	Cardiff

1969

Nov 26th	Maxie Smith	l.pts.8	London

1970

Mar 23rd	Ray Brittle	l.dis.5	London

Allan Ball in action (courtesy of the Western Mail)

19

Dennis Avoth

Dennis Avoth, younger brother of Eddie, was born in Cardiff on October 25th, 1947. He enjoyed a successful amateur career and represented Wales at international level. In 1967, he became Welsh ABA Heavyweight Champion and in 1971 completed the double by becoming Heavyweight Champion of Wales in the professional ranks.

His decision to turn professional came about somewhat unexpectedly. Dennis recalls that he got a telephone call at work from his father, Jack telling him that both Roy John and Allan Ball had decided to turn professional with Eddie Thomas, so Dennis also decided to take the plunge and duly signed professional forms at the Royal Hotel in Cardiff. He was guided by Eddie for the first three years of his career but then decided that his father, Jack, should take over the managerial reins. By this time, Jack was already looking after younger brother Les, a middleweight, who had his first professional contest at Bethnal Green in September, 1969. He was so supportive of their efforts that he erected a boxing ring in the garden to help his sons. Eventually, the three brothers would share the distinction of having appeared at the National Sporting Club.

Dennis Avoth began his professional career on September 14th, 1967 at the World Sporting Club in London stopping Doyley Brown in the fifth round. He drew his next contest in Leicester against Barry Rodney but then went on to stop Paul Brown in the fifth round at Brighton. His first professional contest in Wales was at Aberavon on November 28th when he beat Bert Johnson on points over six rounds on the undercard of the contest between Carl Gizzi and Hubert Hilton. His final contest of the year was at Leicester, where he beat Charlie White on points, again over the six round distance.

On January 22nd, 1968 he appeared at the National Sporting Club for the first time beating Paul Brown on points over eight rounds. He was back in London in February beating Terry Feeley on points, this time at the World Sporting Club.

Two weeks later he was back in action at Northampton against Charlie White, but this was to be the first of four defeats he was to suffer in 1968. His points loss to Terry Daly came on a show at Wembley on April 9th on a bill advertised as "Cavalcade of Champions", promoted by Harry Levene. On the bill, Howard Winstone beat Jimmy Anderson and the show also featured British Champions Ralph Charles and John McCluskey against foreign opposition.

Dennis was much busier in 1969 and was generally successful. In his seventh fight of the year however, he lost on points over eight rounds to future British Lightheavyweight and Heavyweight Champion, Bunny Johnson at Solihull. This was to be the first clash in their three fight series.

On July 7th, Dennis took part in a Heavyweight Competition promoted by Jack Solomons at the World Sporting Club. Solomons had used this idea several times over the years and contests were fought over three rounds. Dennis beat Obe Hepburn and Billy Wynter to reach the final, where he was stopped by Danny McAlinden in the first round. McAlinden would later come to Merthyr to prepare with Eddie Thomas for his contest with Jack Bodell, which saw the Irishman crowned as British Heavyweight Champion.

On paper, Dennis Avoth did not enjoy much success in 1970, his solitary win coming against Terry Feeley, but defeats came over eight rounds at Wembley against Peter Boddington, the former ABA Heavyweight Champion and another defeat followed at the hands of Bunny Johnson on points over ten rounds at Aberavon.

Dennis managed to turn things around in 1971 winning all five contests. He boxed well at Solihull to beat old foe Bunny Johnson on points over eight rounds and on October 11th, he beat former stablemate Carl Gizzi for the Welsh Heavyweight Title at the National Sporting Club. This was a contest which Dennis was determined to win, feeling he had something to prove, and he emerged as the victor on points over ten rounds on the card of referee Joe Morgan, who was himself being assessed for upgrading to "Star Class". Working with Joe was always a pleasure. Our scores were always remarkably similar and I think we both looked for the same things in a fight. In my opinion, Joe was desperately unlucky not to make the top flight as an official. He became despondent and resigned as a referee, and this decision was a huge loss to boxing in Wales.

On November 9th, Dennis forced Guinea Roger to retire in the fifth round, the Nigerian of course, having boxed brother Eddie, and he ended the year with a points win over Brian Jewitt at Bristol.

The following year, 1972 brought a solitary victory and five defeats. In February he was knocked out by former stablemate Roger Tighe and in his next fight was stopped in six rounds by Reading's Les Stevens. He then defended his Welsh title successfully in London when he beat Del Phillips on points over ten rounds. Dennis then lost two fights in succession against Frank Carpenter and ended the year with a points defeat over eight rounds in London at the hands of up and coming Swindon prospect Eddie Neilson.

Dennis began 1973 with a win over former opponent Guinea Roger but on April 19th he lost on points to future British Lightheavyweight Champion Tim Wood in

London. He was beaten again by Eddie Neilson, but on June 27th, Dennis successfully defended his Welsh Heavyweight title against Gene Innocent of Cardiff. The fight took place in Swansea and Dennis retained over ten rounds.

There was to be just one more contest. On August 1st he was knocked out by Phil Matthews in the first round in Cardiff and Dennis subsequently retired. The bitter irony of this defeat was that Matthews had been guided to a British title challenge against Bunny Sterling by Eddie Thomas.

In September 2003, the Welsh Ex-Boxers' Association decided to present Dennis Avoth with a championship belt in recognition of his status as Welsh Heavyweight Champion. It was clearly an emotional day for the Avoth family with brothers Eddie and Les in attendance. The presentation was made by Terry Downes, the former Middleweight Champion of the World and from a personal point of view, it gave me great pleasure to be involved in this gesture, which was thoroughly deserved. Dennis competed with the best British heavyweights of his time and was perhaps unlucky not to make the breakthrough on the British title scene.

Dennis Avoth

Born: Cardiff, October 25th, 1947
Welsh ABA Heavyweight Champion, 1967
Welsh International
Heavyweight Champion of Wales

Professional Record

1967
Sep 14th	Doyley Brown	w.rsf.5	London
Oct 9th	Barry Rodney	d.6	Leicester
Oct 22nd	Paul Brown	w.rsf.5	Brighton
Nov 28th	Bert Johnson	w.pts.6	Aberavon
Dec 11th	Charlie White	w.pts.6	Leicester

1968
Jan 22nd	Paul Brown	w.pts.8	London
Feb 12th	Terry Feeley	w.pts.6	London
Feb 27th	Charlie White	l.pts.8	Northampton
Apr 9th	Terry Daly	l.pts.6	Wembley
May 12th	Vic Moore	l.rsf.7	London
Nov 27th	Charlie White	l.pts.6	Cardiff

1969
Jan 23rd	Charlie White	w.pts.8	Dunstable
Feb 3rd	George Dulaire	w.pts.8	London
Feb 24th	Obe Hepburn	d.8	London
Mar 10th	Jack Cotes	w.pts.6	Bristol
Mar 24th	George Dulaire	w.pts.6	London
Apr 28th	Jack Cotes	w.pts.6	London
May 7th	Bunny Johnson	l.pts.8	Solihull
Jul 2nd	Del Phillips	d.8	Cardiff
Jul 7th	Obe Hepburn	w.pts.3	London
Jul 7th	Billy Wynter	w.pts.3	London
Jul 7th	Dan McAlinden	l.rsf.1	London
	(Final, Heavyweight Comp at WSC)		
Sep 29th	Billy Aird	l.pts.6	London

1970
Jan 12th	Charlie White	l.pts.8	London
Feb 10th	Terry Feeley	w.rsf.4	London
Mar 9th	Cliff Field	l.rsf.7	London
Jun 22nd	Del Phillips	l.pts.10	Swansea
	(Final Elim, Welsh Heavyweight Title)		
Sep 8th	Peter Boddington	l.pts.8	Wembley
Oct 19th	Bunny Johnson	l.pts.10	Aberavon

1971
Jul 5th	Brian Hall	w.pts.6	London
Sep 22nd	Bunny Johnson	w.pts.8	Solihull
Oct 11th	Carl Gizzi	w.pts.10	London
	(Welsh Heavyweight Title)		
Nov 9th	Guinea Roger	w.rtd.5	Wolverhampton
Nov 29th	Brian Jewitt	w.pts.8	Bristol

1972
Feb 14th	Roger Tighe	l.ko.6	London
Mar 27th	Les Stevens	l.rsf.6	Reading
Apr 24th	Del Phillips	w.pts.10	London
	(Welsh Heavyweight Title)		
Jun 27th	Frank Carpenter	l.pts.8	Birmingham
Oct 24th	Frank Carpenter	l.pts.8	Birmingham
Nov 27th	Eddie Neilson	l.pts.8	London

1973
Feb 5th	Guinea Roger	w.pts.8	Swansea
Apr 19th	Tim Wood	l.pts.8	Wolverhampton
Apr 30th	Eddie Neilson	l.pts.8	London
Jun 27th	Gene Innocent	w.pts.10	Swansea
	(Welsh Heavyweight Title)		
Aug 1st	Phil Matthews	l.ko.1	Cardiff

Dennis Avoth: Welsh Heavyweight Champion

20

Recollections of the Stable

After setting up gyms in local pubs Eddie Thomas eventually took over the old snooker hall in Penydarren High Street, almost opposite the Co-op butcher shop where Howard Winstone and Don James worked as delivery boys.

The building always seemed to have a faded look about it though the ground floor did briefly take on a new lease of life when Eddie's wife Kay opened a dress shop and hairdressing salon, but the venture was shortlived.

I became a regular visitor to the gym with my father, Emrys. The first striking feature was the old flight of wooden stairs which Eddie always ran up, taking two steps at a time and when he arrived he would often be late and he would sometimes be covered in coal dust after his day's work at the mine.

Climbing the stairs, I was always aware of the fascinating combination of sounds percolating down from the "sweat box". There was always the whir of the skipping ropes and the sound of the rope beating on the wooden floor. There was the thud of the heavy bag and the repetitive sound of the speedball. On reaching the top of the stairs, all these sounds made sense, with each of the boxers present preparing themselves for the rigours of the ring. It was a genuine old fashioned gym but the toilets were best avoided and the effectiveness of the showers depended on the leaking roof and how heavily it was raining!

Eddie could not have managed without the assistance of a dedicated group of friends. Ronnie Newton always seemed to be doing odd jobs about the place. Dennis Donovan would be throwing the medicine ball at assorted stomachs as the boxers completed their mat exercises and he would then often double up as the masseur. Danny Reardon and Billy Long would keep a watchful eye on the clock as they timed boxers going through their various activities, be it shadow boxing or working on the bag, and the ever cool Roy Sier always seemed to take particular care of Howard Winstone.

Dr Kevin Mangan would visit frequently to keep an eye on the boxers and to attend to their needs. Local poet Charles Jones would often spend time there and another regular was Billy O'Donovan, usually still wearing his white butcher's hat. And of course, there were always fight fans casting an eye over their heroes.

In spite of all the hard work there was always a great sense of fun about the place.

There would be friendly banter between Howard Winstone and Eddie Avoth. Dai Harris could always be relied upon to see the funny side of things while Glyn Davies also had a wicked sense of humour, but I shall always remember Gerry Banwell as the resident comedian while Eddie Thomas was often on the receiving end of numerous practical jokes.

Sparring sessions were always a pleasure to watch, with those between Winstone and Ken Buchanan being a treat for the purists, though I know Howard did not like facing Ken towards the end of a long session.

It is during these sessions that a boxer hones his skills and occasionally, rounds at the gym would become pretty torrid, but Eddie would always be on hand to issue the instruction to "cool it", or even to end a round early to defuse a situation. He disliked seeing his boxers involved in what might be called gym wars, because over a career, these can be damaging.

There were regular visitors to the gym for sparring sessions and these included Dai Corp, who boxed many rounds with Howard while I think it is fair to say that Billy Thomas sacrificed his own career because he was happy to work as Howard's sparring partner. Billy had beaten both Gerald Jones and Glyn Davies but he was great fun to be with and he enjoyed working with Howard. Billy even went to Mexico with Howard for the third contest against Vicente Saldivar and was persuaded to spar with Ruben Olivares, without being fully aware of whom he was working with. The word is that legendary fight manager and promoter George Parnassus asked Eddie if Billy was prepared to spar with Ruben. Billy agreed and soon began to fancy the job. He started to throw some heavy shots with Olivares shaking his head and muttering "No". Eventually, Olivares tired of this and landed a shot which ended Billy's ambitions rather abruptly! Billy was a great character but sadly died in 2003 after a long battle against cancer.

Another visitor was Colin Lake. He always got on well with Howard and was an excellent sparring partner. In February 1969 Colin boxed Jimmy Anderson for the British Junior – Lightweight title but was stopped in seven rounds. Jimmy Anderson became the first champion in this newly introduced weight category in February 1968, but in his next contest lost on points over ten rounds to Howard Winstone at Wembley. After retiring from boxing, Colin Lake became a highly respected trainer and took Colin Dunne to the WBU Lightweight title. He is still involved in the game and attends boxing functions the length and breadth of the country.

Mickey Laud was another regular visitor, sparring with both Howard and Ken Buchanan. He came from St Ives and was the brother of Monty Laud, who was ABA Flyweight Champion in 1963, and Winston Laud. Mickey was a solid professional whose work in the gym was greatly valued.

George Evans, the son of Howard's first trainer Billy, would often turn up at the gym. He was a lightweight, managed by Cardiff's Mac Williams and would frequently spar with Howard and some of the others. In December, 1972, shortly after beginning my referee's scoring tests, I met Mac and George at Leeds Town Hall, where George beat local favourite Tommy Sobles on points over eight rounds. After I returned to Wales in 1975, both Mac and George were extremely helpful in my development as a referee with Mac allowing me to patrol the ring in Cardiff with Billy Waith and Pat Thomas, and George allowing me to visit his gym at Abercanaid so that I could share the ring with Merthyr lightweight Johnny Wall, Ceri Collins and others.

Eddie always insisted on boxers cooling off properly and it was at such times that I enjoyed chatting to Eddie Avoth and Carl Gizzi, and I can remember, one night, talking to a shattered Roger Tighe after a particularly demanding workout, though I have to say that Eddie Thomas was often frustrated by Roger's laid back approach. I also remember talking to Chic Calderwood, the British and Empire Lightheavyweight Champion from Craigneuk, Scotland, who trained at the gym for his contest with Freddie Cross at Porthcawl on July 24th, 1964. This was on the undercard of Brian Curvis' title defence against Johnny Cooke with Chic winning on points after eight rounds.

Calderwood was one of my favourite boxers at the time. In the calm of the changing room he came over as a quiet, sincere person, though he dominated the Lightheavyweight scene in Britain for much of the sixties. He beat the likes of Yolande Pompey, Willie Pastrano and Johnny Persol, but lost to Henry Hank in Detroit. When his world title opportunity came along he was unlucky in having to travel to San Juan to face Jose Torres, a fine champion, and I can still recall the feeling of great sadness when Chic Calderwood was killed in a road crash on November 13th, 1966.

Chic never lost his British and Empire titles in the ring though had to forfeit them when he served a prison sentence for assault at the end of 1963. I found it hard to believe that the person I met in 1964 had been through the experience of prison and I was delighted to see him regain the British title later that year.

For a time, Eddie had some of his stable lodging at the Crawshays Arms, a pub in my home village of Cefn Coed and Carl Gizzi, Eddie Avoth and Ken Buchanan would sometimes play snooker during the afternoon at Cefn Coed Workmens' Club at the top of the street where I lived. Ken was rather luckier on the lodgings front and from his early days in Merthyr was looked after by Myfanwy, mother of Phil Jones and almost forty years on Ken and Phil remain great friends.

Another of Myfanwy's distinguished lodgers was Joe Bugner, who stayed with her while training in Merthyr during the early part of his career. Joe became British, Commonwealth and European Heavyweight Champion when he beat Henry Cooper at Wembley on March 16th, 1971 but never really won over the hearts of British fight fans and was never forgiven for having beaten Henry, who, in his seventies, remains the people's champion. Joe Bugner acquitted himself well against Joe Frazier and twice went the distance with Muhammad Ali, but fight fans found his cautious approach frustrating.

Roadwork around Pontsarn was always something of a test and I can remember Eddie asking my father to have a pair of weights made by the blacksmith at the colliery where he worked so that Carl Gizzi could carry these in his hands during his early morning runs. I have a picture of Carl running up the notorious "Sanatorium Hill" with the weights clearly seen in his hands and Eddie following closely behind in his car to ensure that there was no shirking.

When Howard set up training camp in West Wales for his second contest with Vicente Saldivar at Ninian Park, Sandy Saddler appeared, supposedly in an advisory capacity. Saddler will always be remembered for his epic battles with Willy Pep and their contests are the stuff of legend. That being said, I cannot believe that Eddie needed any advice on Howard's preparation at that stage of his career.

Another familiar face around the gym was the old trainer Archie Rule who had been associated with many top class fighters and who always went about his work quietly and efficiently. He always seemed to be in his shirt sleeves with his trousers held up by the familiar pair of braces, a figure from a bygone age.

Howard Davies was another frequent visitor to the gym. He eventually became known as "Howard the Back" when it became clear that he had a remarkable gift for sorting out the back and joint problems of many local people. He was one of those characters who always seemed to be smiling.

During the 1960's, Les Roberts, the matchmaker at the National Sporting Club became a regular visitor to Merthyr. He and Eddie developed a close working relationship and stable members boxed regularly at the Club. Over the years Welsh boxers have frequently become favourites at the NSC going back as far as the days of Jim Driscoll, Tom Thomas, Freddie Welsh and Jimmy Wilde and now it was the turn of Winstone, Avoth, Buchanan, Gizzi and all the other Merthyr trained boxers to enjoy similar popularity.

The relationship between Eddie and Les finally turned sour. I never had the opportunity of discussing this with Eddie, but as my refereeing career developed I met Les many times and we often had time for lengthy conversations. He was always the dour Yorkshireman and he frequently gave me pieces of good advice relating to refereeing, but he had no time for trivial things. He maintained that they had fallen out over a financial matter, and so, sadly, a successful partnership came to an end.

Les invited me to the National Sporting Club on a couple of occasions after I became a referee and on my second visit, my father was also invited to come along. He and Les had been friends for many years and he often drove Les around when he came down to Wales for Eddie's promotions. My father and I enjoyed many memorable nights at the boxing, but our visit to the NSC with its great sense of history and tradition gave him enormous pleasure.

With Eddie and his boxers being such regular visitors to London he stayed frequently at the Regent Palace Hotel in Piccadilly. Merthyr fight fans adopted the hotel as their headquarters whenever they were in London for Howard Winstone's important contests and there were some great nights there when Howard was involved in championship action. The place would be filled with song, and there always seemed to be time for a quick visit to the "Regent" before starting the long journey home. It was a place that became special for many of us and members of the fight fraternity always seemed to congregate there on the big occasions.

Joe Bugner was not the only heavyweight visitor to Merthyr. Promoter Jack Solomons sent Danny McAlinden to the town to prepare for his British title fight against Jack Bodell, and Don James often tells the story of how the Irishman was almost reduced to tears by the very sight of "Sanatorium Hill".

To see Eddie at work on the pads with his protégés was an unforgettable experience. Here was the maestro at work and this was where he sharpened their technical skills. In later years when boxing was generally thought to be in decline Eddie often lamented the fact that there were few good teachers around and when I see some of our present day trainers work on the pads with their boxers I can see exactly what Eddie meant. I really wonder whether some of them understand what it is they are trying to achieve.

Eddie had perfected the art of bringing a boxer to the peak of physical fitness and would always give specific instructions as to how many rounds a boxer should complete on the various activities. He would stipulate the time to be spent skipping and would then indicate the number of rounds on the heavy bag, shadow boxing, sparring and the speedball. He knew instinctively when his boxers needed to ease off and was an expert in tapering off the exercise during those last few days leading up to a contest and I often felt that what he said to boxers during this time was possibly more important than what they did because he was trying to ensure that they were not only physically fit, but mentally prepared for the job in hand. His use of psychology showed how completely he knew and understood the needs of each of his fighters.

It was always a special pleasure for me to see Eddie himself round off a training session with a few minutes on the speedball. Even in his forties, with his fighting days long gone, it was clear that here was an artist at work.

Don James once expressed the view that for Eddie's boxers, the gym was their college, the place where they received their education. They could have had no finer place of learning and no finer teacher and I shall always treasure my memories of the gym and of the special people who made it what it was. There can be no doubt that during the 1960s, this was the most successful boxing stable in Britain.